INTERMEDIATE 2
Hospitality
course notes

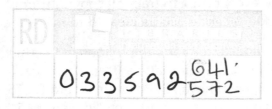

✕ Alastair MacGregor ✕

Text © 2008 Alastair MacGregor
Design and layout © 2008 Leckie & Leckie
Cover photo © Gallo Images/Gettyimages
Cover design by Caleb Rutherford

02/180209

ISBN 978-1-84372-476-6

Published by
Leckie & Leckie Ltd
3rd Floor, 4 Queen Street, Edinburgh EH2 1JE
Phone: 0131 220 6831   Fax: 0131 225 9987
enquiries@leckieandleckie.co.uk   www.leckieandleckie.co.uk

Special thanks to
Project One Publishing Solutions (project management and editing)
The Partnership Publishing Solutions (design and page layout)
Ellustration (illustrations)

A CIP Catalogue record for this book is available from the British Library.

® Leckie & Leckie is a registered trademark.
Leckie & Leckie is a division of Huveaux PLC

Leckie & Leckie makes every effort to ensure that all paper used in our books is made from wood pulp obtained from well-managed forests, controlled sources and recycled wood or fibre.

Acknowledgements
Leckie & Leckie has made every effort to trace all copyright holders. If any have been inadvertently overlooked, Leckie & Leckie will be pleased to make the necessary arrangements.

Leckie & Leckie would like to thank the following for their permission to reproduce their material free of charge:
Sandy Austin (p. 75, cherimoya), R. Philip Bouchard (p. 75, guanabana), Rachel Johnson (p. 61, taro root), Nga Nguyen (p. 61, longan).

Leckie & Leckie would like to thank the following for their permission to reproduce their material:
Alamy Images (p. 101, granadilla; p. 102, starfruit and tamarillo; p. 104, yam; p. 120, gugelhopf).

CONTENTS

Introduction

Welcome to *Intermediate 2 Hospitality (Practical Cookery) Course Notes*. This book will help you as your progress your way through your Intermediate 2 Hospitality: Practical Cookery course.

This book provides you with full coverage of all the content and knowledge that is required for the course and is designed to help you:

- develop your practical cooking skills
- further develop your skills in the use of culinary equipment
- amend and adapt recipes
- practise your numeracy skills through food costing
- develop an awareness of international cuisine.

The chapters of the book are arranged to cover the main areas of course content. Practical preparation and cooking tips and notes on the importance of safety and hygiene are included throughout the book.

Chapter 1: Cookery Skills

This chapter provides an insight into the professional kitchen and gives an overview of the cookery skills required in the professional kitchen. It combines both information and activities that will allow you to gain an understanding of the main terms and definitions used in the professional kitchen, the range of equipment that you might need to use when undertaking some food preparation techniques, as well as providing an overview of simple presentation and garnishing techniques.

Chapter 2: Food Preparation for Healthy Eating

This chapter looks at the responsibilities of the professional chef in relation to providing food which meets current health guidelines. It provides up-to-date information on healthy eating guidelines and how to ensure a balanced diet. A range of activities enable you to adapt standard recipes to meet current health guidelines.

Chapter 3: Foods and Recipes from Around the World

This chapter provides an overview of some of the most popular international cuisines, specifically looking at the factors that affect food choice and examining some of the key ingredients from each country. It also provides recipes from all of these countries. These recipes can be tried at home, or in class. The countries discussed are: China, France, Mexico, Morocco and Greece.

Chapter 4: Key Ingredients

This chapter describes key characteristics of some of the key ingredients and foods that are used in professional kitchens, at home and abroad.

Course assessment

Intermediate 2 Hospitality: Practical Cookery does not have a final written examination, but you will be assessed in the component units that make up the course awards:

- Food Preparation for Healthy Eating
- Foods of the World
- Practical Cookery Skills for the Hospitality Industry.

Your course assessment is based on a practical assignment undertaken under controlled conditions. The assignment will be set by the Scottish Qualifications Authority and will:

- incorporate a range of techniques, equipment, processes and ingredients
- involve the planning and preparation of four portions of three different dishes within a $2\frac{1}{2}$ hour period and will include at least one healthy food dish and one dish from a specified country.

The practical assignment is worth 100 marks and will be assessed by your class teacher.

How to use this book

This book has a clear, easy-to-read layout with a number of features designed to help you understand the course.

For you to do   This feature provides you with a range of tasks and activities designed to test your knowledge of the content of the book. This feature also helps as a revision and consolidation activity.

Leckie & Leckie Learning Lab   This feature indicates when activities and web links mentioned in *For you to do* activities are listed on the Leckie & Leckie Learning Lab page. To find these, go to: www.leckieandleckie.co.uk, click on the Learning Lab button and navigate to the Intermediate 2 Hospitality Course Notes page.

Word bank   This feature explains or defines some of the important terms used in the book.

Hints and Tips   This feature provides you with some important points that will help you with your studies. These hints and tips will be about your course content or about steps that you can take to improve your practical skills. Some tips relate specifically with to healthy eating and/or food safety and hygiene.

Answers   Answers to the *For you to do* activities are given on pages 122–125.

Glossary   A glossary is given on pages 126–128, making it easy for you to quickly look up definitions and explanations

CHAPTER 1
COOKERY SKILLS

Kitchen Organisation

Many large kitchens are organised by what is known as a **partie** or **brigade system**. This system for organising roles and responsibilities in the kitchen was established by a famous French chef, restaurateur and food writer, called Auguste Escoffier.

The typical brigade system is:

1 Head Chef – Chef de Cuisine

2 Second Chef – Sous Chef

3 Section Heads – Chefs de Partie

- Larder Chef – le Garde-Manger
  - Cold Work Chef – le Chef du Froid
  - Hors d'Oeuvre Chef – le Hors d'Oeuvrier
  - Butcher – le Boucher

  These three chefs come under the Garde-Manger.

- Sauce Chef – le Saucier
- Roast Chef – le Rôtisseur
- Fish Chef – le Poissonnier
- Vegetable Chef – l'Entremettier
- Soup Chef – le Potager
- Pastry Chef – le Pâtissier
- Baker – le Boulanger
- Relief Chef – le Tournant
- Staff Chef – le Communard
- Night or Duty Chef – le Chef du Nuit or le Chef de Garde
- Breakfast Chef – le Chef du Petit Déjeuner
- Carver – le Trancheur
- Grill Chef – le Grillardin

4 Assistant Chefs – Commis chefs – big sections could have first, second and third commis chefs

5 Apprentice – l'Apprenti

The flowchart opposite summarises the organisation in a typical kitchen.

The brigade system will vary, depending on the size of the kitchen. The biggest factors affecting how a kitchen is organised are the menu and the system used to prepare and present the menu items. Organisation and efficiency are very important. Everyone needs to know what they should be doing, and how and when they should be doing it. This is what Escoffier tried to achieve with his system.

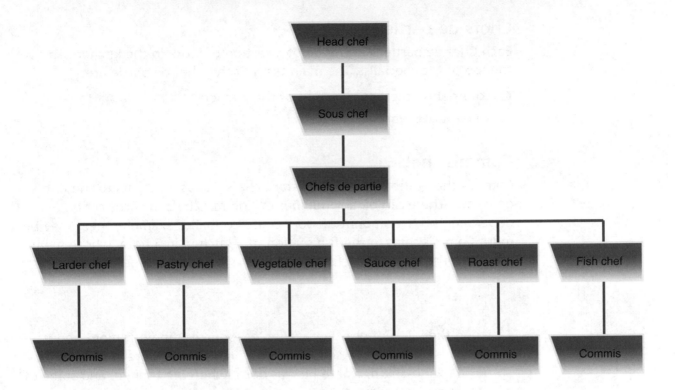

Roles of the Chefs

Head chef

The Head chef is in charge of the kitchen and is responsible for allocating the work between the different kitchen sections and for ensuring that results meet the expected standard. The main tasks of the Head chef are:

- to organise the kitchen
- to devise the menu
- to order food items
- to undertake costing to meet required profit levels
- to recruit staff and supervise the kitchen
- to advise as required.

This is a very important role as the skill and expertise of the Head chef affects the success and **reputation** of the whole kitchen.

Sous chef

The Sous chef is the assistant to the Head chef. A good Sous chef will have expert knowledge of all sections of the kitchen. The main tasks of the Sous chef are:

- to take over when the Head chef is off duty
- to supervise the work in the kitchen to ensure it is done as the Head chef requires.

In large kitchens there may be a number of Sous chefs, each with specific **responsibilities**, for example, the grill room or banquets.

Chefs de partie

Each Chef de partie is in charge of a section of work in the kitchen. This is the job of the specialist. The main tasks of the Chef de partie are:

- to organise their own section of the kitchen
- to **deputise** work to assistants.

Commis chefs

Commis chefs, also known as assistant chefs, act as assistants to the Chefs de partie. There can be any number of Commis chefs in each section, depending on the amount of work to be done. For example, there may be more Commis chefs in the fish section of a kitchen in a hotel whose menu offers a large selection of fish dishes.

For you to do

1 Using the internet or other available resources, find out more about Auguste Escoffier. You should specifically find out more about: his date of birth and death, where he was born, where he trained, and some of the books he wrote.

Tip: type 'escoffier history' into an internet search engine.

Mise-en-place

Another French term that you might come across in relation to kitchen organisation is **mise-en-place**. This means preparing food ingredients and equipment before service. Much of the preparation is done throughout the day – for example, meat, fish and cold dishes can be prepared and stored in refrigerators until needed at service time. The cooking and finishing can then be done quickly by skilled chefs to be ready when the customer requires their food.

Kitchen Partie Activities

Let's look at each kitchen partie and examine the activities that would be undertaken by each.

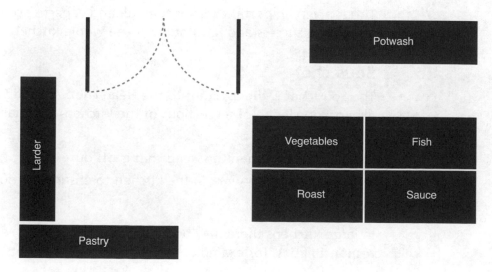

Potwash

Kitchen porters are responsible for general cleaning duties in the kitchen. In some large kitchens, porters may assist the chefs, for example, to prepare breadcrumbs, peel vegetables and chop herbs. The kitchen may have a scullery assistant who has responsibility for collecting and washing all the pots and pans and returning them to the correct place in the kitchen.

Larder partie

This section is mainly concerned with preparing food which is needed by other parties. Prepared items must be sent in the right quantities to the right section at the right time for cooking. This section is responsible for the preparation of:

- poultry and game
- meat
- fish
- cold savoury dishes – prepared and garnished ready for serving
- canapés and sandwiches
- hors d'oeuvres and salads.

Vegetable partie

This section is responsible for cooking all vegetable and starchy/flour-based (**farinaceous**) dishes, specifically the preparation and cooking of:

- vegetables and potatoes
- soups
- stocks
- vegetable savouries
- eggs
- farinaceous dishes, for example, pancakes.

Fish partie

This section is responsible for cooking all fish dishes, specifically the cooking and presentation of hot fish and shellfish dishes, including:

- cooking of fish and shellfish for cold presentation
- preparation of hot fish sauces
- preparation of, for example, Béchamel sauce.

Sauce partie

The section prepares sauces for meat dishes, entrées, and all meat, game and poultry dishes which are not roasted or grilled, specifically the cooking of:

- all made-up dishes such as stews and pies, braised, boiled and sautéd dishes, etc.
- meat, poultry and game sauces
- garnishes for their dishes.

Roast partie

This section is responsible for roasting, frying and grilling, specifically the cooking of:

- roast and grilled meat, poultry and game
- grilled and deep-fried fish
- other deep-fried foods including potatoes
- garnishes for roast dishes, for example, grilled mushrooms, tomatoes
- Yorkshire puddings
- meat gravy.

Pastry partie

This section is responsible for making all sweets and pastries, specifically the preparation and cooking of:

- all hot and cold sweets
- cakes and pastries
- items required by other sections, such as vol au vent cases, pastry covers for pies, etc.
- ice cream
- petit fours
- bakery goods.

Canapé: *a small, thin biscuit or piece of bread which has savoury food on top, such as cheese, fish or meat, and is served with drinks, especially at a party.*

Deputise: *do something in the place of another person, particularly by a person whose rank is immediately below that of the leader of an organisation.*

Farinaceous: *flour-based.*

Hors d'oeuvre: *a small, savoury dish eaten at the start of a meal.*

Partie: *a system that is used to organise the work in a kitchen to make the best use of time and resources, with each section having responsibility for preparing and/or cooking specific types of dishes.*

Petit four: *a small cake or biscuit, usually served at the end of a meal with coffee.*

Reputation: *the general opinion people have about someone or something, based on past behaviour or character.*

Responsibility: *the control and authority someone has over something or someone, and the duty of taking care of it or them.*

Weighing and Measuring

The proper weighing and measuring of ingredients is important to successful cooking and baking. Many foods can be affected by too much or too little of certain ingredients. Inaccurate measuring or weighing can affect:

- the flavour of food, for example, adding too much salt to potatoes and making them taste salty
- the texture of food, for example, adding too much flour to a cake mix and making it very dry
- the appearance of food, for example, adding too much colouring to an icing mix.

When cooking you will need to measure and weigh:

- dry ingredients such as sugar, flour and spices
- wet ingredients such as water, wine and stock.

You will use the following measuring equipment in the kitchen:

- scales (also called 'manual scales')
- digital scales
- measuring jugs and cups
- measuring spoons.

You will usually find that weights and measures given in recipes are provided as metric measurements. Metric measures (and their abbreviations) include:

- grams (g)
- kilograms (kg)
- millilitres (ml)
- litres (l).

However, some older recipe books will provide weights and measures using different measurement systems, such as cups, ounces and pounds. It is important that you always use metric weights and measures. Use the conversion chart on the Leckie & Leckie Learning Lab page to convert these older types of weights and measures to metric weights and measures.

Handy Measures

In a professional kitchen, many experienced chefs do not always measure all ingredients. This is because they have had lots of practice and can judge weights and measurements well. Many will also use **handy measures** to help with judging weights and measures.

Handy measures are a quick way to measure ingredients without having to use scales or particular measuring spoons. Handy measures are used for dry ingredients. The table on page 12 lists some handy spoon measures.

Handy measures	
1 tablespoon = 3 teaspoons	1 level tablespoon = 15ml
1 dessertspoon = 2 teaspoons	1 level teaspoon = 5ml

A chef will use a tablespoon to measure out dry ingredients, for example, flour and sugar. Unless specified otherwise, this usually means a rounded tablespoon.

A **rounded tablespoon** is where you take a tablespoon of the dry ingredient and the amount of the ingredient that is held **in the bowl** of the spoon is about the same as the amount **above the top** of the spoon.

A **heaped tablespoon** means that you put as much ingredient on to the spoon as you can without it falling off.

A **level tablespoon** is where you place the ingredient on to a spoon and scrape a knife across the edges of the spoon, levelling the ingredient with the top edge of the spoon.

Use this table when measuring about 25g of the ingredients listed.

Ingredient	No. level tablespoons	Ingredient	No. level tablespoons
Breadcrumbs (fresh)	6	Icing sugar (sifted)	3
Cheese (grated)	5	Porridge oats	4
Cocoa powder	4	Rice	2
Flour	3	Salt	1
Honey/Syrup/Jam	1	Sugar (granulated)	2

Handy measures when measuring fat

Margarine and butter come in 250g blocks. Just lightly mark the top of the butter into five equal blocks and you have five 50g blocks ready to cut.

Hints and tips

It is important that you always use weighing and measuring equipment for wet and dry ingredients. This will help to ensure a good end product.

Measuring Terminology

Other weighing and measuring terms you should be familiar with include:

- **dash:** a small amount of a dry ingredient; a dash of a liquid is about three drops
- **dot:** to scatter small pieces of butter over the top of a prepared dish
- **dust:** to sprinkle food lightly with flour, sugar or other dry ingredient
- **pinch:** the amount of a dry ingredient (for example, salt) that you can pick up between your thumb and forefinger
- **scant:** less than enough.

For you to do

2 Suggest how you might measure the following ingredients if you didn't have measuring scales or a measuring jug:

    a   100g plain flour   b   100g sugar

    c   5ml lemon juice   d   25ml lemon juice

    e   125g butter   f   50g grated cheese

    g   2.5ml paprika.

Preparation Techniques

Professional chefs undergo extensive training in order to produce quality food. They use many different food preparation techniques to ensure that the products that they produce not only look good, but also smell and taste good. This section introduces you to some of the terminology and related techniques that chefs use.

Assemble

Description

Decorate: *to add edible items, usually to sweets, to make them look attractive.*

Garnish: *to decorate food, usually savoury, with a small amount of different food to make it attractive.*

Food assembly really comes at the end of the food production sequence as it involves putting the finished dish together. The assembly of the dish requires an eye for detail as this affects the appearance of the prepared food. Even the best cooked food will not look appetising if it is not well assembled. Once a dish is assembled, it may still need to be **garnished** or **decorated**.

Equipment required

The type of cooking equipment required for the assembly of food will vary depending on the type of dish you are making but examples include:

- serving dish
- serving spoon or ladle
- palette or fish knife.

For you to do

3 Visit the Expert Village website which shows the process of assembling vegan spring rolls. What equipment was used to assemble the spring rolls?

Links to this site and other websites relating to Intermediate 2 Hospitality can be found at: www.leckieandleckie.co.uk by clicking on the Learning Lab button and navigating to the Intermediate 2 Hospitality Course Notes page.

Blanch

Description

Blanching is the process of immersing food into boiling water in order to cook it slightly. The food is then 'refreshed' by immersing it into ice-cold water to stop the cooking process. A chef would blanch foods for a number of reasons:

- to preserve the natural colour of vegetables, which can be lost through cooking
- to stop any chemical changes in the food before freezing, for example, to prevent fruit and vegetables from ripening during the freezing period
- to preserve the nutritive value of the food
- to preserve the flavour of the food.

Blanching is mainly used to part-cook vegetables for reheating and serving at a later stage. This method of blanching uses water as described above.

Chips are also blanched prior to cooking, normally in fat which is at 165°C. This starts the cooking process but does not fully cook or colour the potatoes. They are then deep-fried in fat at a much hotter temperature before being served.

Equipment required

A pan is required for blanching, but the size and type of pan depends on the type and quantity of food being blanched. A slotted spoon, colander, sieve or wire basket are needed to remove the food once blanching has been completed.

Hints and tips

Blanched vegetables should be covered, labelled and stored in a refrigerator, for no more than 48 hours, until ready for reheating and service.

For you to do

4 What advice would you give to the following question appearing on an online food website?

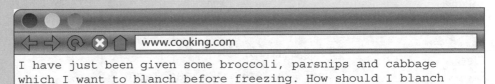

www.cooking.com

I have just been given some broccoli, parsnips and cabbage which I want to blanch before freezing. How should I blanch these vegetables and for how long?

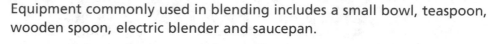

Blend

Description

To blend means to mix food together evenly. This normally describes mixing a starchy powder (for example, corn flour) with a liquid (for example, water) before being used in sauces and gravies.

Equipment required

Equipment commonly used in blending includes a small bowl, teaspoon, wooden spoon, electric blender and saucepan.

In commercial kitchens chefs may have to blend large quantities of food. There are professional items of electrical equipment that can be used for this purpose, such as the industrial blender and the hand-held blender.

An industrial blender (left) is useful for making a variety of dishes including smoothies, fresh juice, milkshakes, soups, sauces, breads and dressings.

A hand-held bar or immersion blender (right) can be used directly in pans of boiling liquid. They have a variety of uses, including mixing, blending, making purées, adding air, chopping and grinding small solid items such as coffee beans.

Hints and tips

Take care when using a blender or processor for hot liquids as they can cause a nasty scald.

For you to do

5 Study the recipe below for Mango and Pineapple Frappé and answer the questions that follow.

Mango and Pineapple Frappé

Ingredients

125ml peeled and stoned mango

375ml pineapple juice

125ml canned coconut milk, well shaken

8 large scoops vanilla ice-cream

25ml sweetened whipped cream

toasted coconut, optional

Method

1   Chill four cocktail glasses in a freezer.

2   Purée half the mango in blender until smooth.

3   Add half of all other ingredients except the whipped cream and toasted coconut; blend until just smooth. Do not over-blend or mixture may become too thin.

4   Divide the frappé mixture between the chilled glasses.

5   Repeat blending with remaining ingredients and add to glasses.

6   Top with toasted coconut and whipped cream.

    a   What ingredients are being blended together?

    b   What does the recipe mean by 'over-blending'?

    c   What might happen if the mixture is over-blended?

Chop

Description

Chopping is the process of cutting food into smaller pieces with a sharp knife. This is normally done using a cook's knife.

Equipment required

Chopping requires a chopping board and a suitable knife, for example, a cook's knife (also known as a chef's knife).

Hints and tips

When cutting with a knife these is always a risk of injury. One hand should always be used as a guiding hand to:

■   prevent the item being cut from slipping

■   control the size of the finished item.

The first knuckle of the third finger of the guiding hand should touch the side of the knife blade after each end cut has been made. The guiding hand will then move back; how far it moves back determines the thickness of the next cut.

Did you know that a blunt knife can be more dangerous than a sharp knife? Make sure that all kitchen preparation knives are kept sharp.

Dice

Description

Dicing is the process of cutting food into small, regular-sized cubes. An ingredient like a pepper is first sliced lengthwise and then the slices are cut into long thin strips. These are lined up and cut into cubes.

Equipment required

Dicing requires a chopping board and a suitable knife, for example, a cook's knife.

For you to do

6 Visit the About.com video library website and watch the video clip on how to dice an onion, then answer these questions.

   a What kind of onion did the chef use?

   b Why was the onion left connected at the root end?

   c What types of dishes did the chef suggest the onion could be used for?

Links to this site and other websites relating to Intermediate 2 Hospitality can be found at: www.leckieandleckie.co.uk by clicking on the Learning Lab button and navigating to the Intermediate 2 Hospitality Course Notes page.

Fold

Description

Folding is a gentle way of mixing ingredients such as whipped cream or beaten egg whites into another ingredient without releasing air. A spatula or metal tablespoon is used to gently mix the ingredients together using a figure-of-eight movement with the mixing tool. The process continues until the ingredients are fully combined. Folding is a technique used when making meringues or a whisked sponge.

Equipment required

The equipment used for folding includes a bowl, tablespoon or spatula.

For you to do

7 Visit the You Tube website and watch the video on folding carefully. Then answer these questions.

   a Why do you think that a scoopful of egg whites were folded into the mousse mixture at the start?

   b How do you know when the egg white has been incorporated fully?

Links to this site and other websites relating to Intermediate 2 Hospitality can be found at: www.leckieandleckie.co.uk by clicking on the Learning Lab button and navigating to the Intermediate 2 Hospitality Course Notes page.

Knead

Description

Kneading is a technique used to mix and prepare a bread dough in order to make it into a firm, smooth and pliable (easy to work) dough. This is usually done on a floured board or surface. Kneading is done by a pressing and pushing movement – pressing the dough down with the heels of the hand and then pushing forwards. This process is repeated until the dough is firm, smooth and elastic, and can take 5–15 minutes.

Note: When kneading a pastry or biscuit dough, the kneading process is much shorter and gentler, otherwise the dough becomes stretched and will shrink and/or harden when cooked. When kneading such dough, chefs tend to use fingers rather than the heels of their hands.

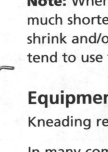

Equipment required

Kneading requires only a floured board and a flour dredger.

In many commercial kitchens, bread dough would be kneaded by a machine that can mix as well as knead the dough. Similarly dough hook attachments can be bought for commercial food processors and planetary mixers. The planetary mixer shown here is a commercial electric whisk.

For you to do

8 Use the internet to find out more about planetary mixers, and answer these questions.

a What is the price range for planetary mixers?

b What types of attachments are available?

c Name some of the different uses of a planetary mixer.

Marinate

Description

Marinating involves placing food into a liquid or paste in order to make the food more tender prior to cooking, or to add flavour. The liquid or paste in which the food is soaked for varying lengths of time is called a **marinade**. A marinade is usually a blend of oil, wine or vinegar, herbs and spices.

Some marinades are used to add flavour and may include an acid (such as lemon juice), herbs and spices. Other marinades are used to make the meat more tender, for example, those containing pineapple. Depending on the dish being made, some marinades will add both flavour and tenderise.

Equipment required

Equipment commonly used for marinating include a dish or bowl for the food to sit in, a lid or cover for the dish, and tablespoon or pastry brush to brush the marinade over food.

9 Visit the Expert Village website, watch the video clip on marinating beef, and then answer these questions.

   a What product was being marinated?

   b What ingredients were used in the marinade?

   c For how long should the beef be marinated?

Pass

Description

Passing involves putting a liquid or purée through a sieve or strainer to make it smooth or to remove lumps. This is also sometimes called straining.

Equipment required

To pass, you need to use a sieve, a fine mesh strainer or a chinois strainer (see page 22).

Purée

Description

To purée is the process of mashing foods until they are smooth and free of lumps. This process can be done by hand, by rubbing through a sieve, or by blitzing in a blender or food processor.

Purée is also a term used for some types of soup, such as lentil soup or a soup thickened with potato or rice.

Equipment required

Equipment commonly used when puréeing includes sieve, food processor, blender or liquidiser.

10 Use the internet or other references to answer these questions.

   a Make a list of ten different types of soup purées.

   b What is the difference between tomato purée, tomato paste and tomato sauce?

Rub in

Description

To rub in is the process of incorporating fat into flour, normally using the fingertips of your hands, until the mixture resembles fine breadcrumbs. Some chefs now use a food processor to rub in because this is a quick method and keeps the ingredients cool which is important.

Rubbing in is a technique used in the preparation of dough for pastry, biscuits and crumble mixes.

Equipment required

Equipment needed for rubbing in includes a round-bladed knife to cut the butter or margarine and a bowl to rub the mixture in. If not rubbing in by hand, other equipment might include a food processor or a pastry blender (useful if, due to poor hand movement, you are unable to rub in using your fingertips).

Hints and tips

When rubbing in, lift the mixture as high as possible and let it fall into the bowl, to incorporate more air. This keeps the mixture light. If the mixture starts to warm up or the fat becomes oily, place it in the fridge for a while to cool the ingredients down a bit.

If your hands feel warm before you start rubbing in, run cold tap water over your wrists for a short time. This will cool down your hands down and prevent them from melting the fat before it is fully rubbed in.

Segment

Description

Segmenting is the process of removing the skin of, for example, citrus fruits, and dividing the flesh into natural wedges. Segmenting is normally done with oranges and grapefruits.

The correct technical name for segmenting a citrus fruit is 'to supreme'. When a chef supremes an orange, they remove the skin, the **pith**, all the **membranes** and the seeds, leaving only the fleshy part of the fruit.

Membrane: *a very thin layer of material surrounding and protecting individual segments of an orange.*
Pith: *white substance between the skin and flesh of a citrus fruit.*

Equipment required

To segment citrus fruit you will need a paring or vegetable knife and a chopping board.

Skin

Description

Skinning is the process of removing the outer skin of a food, for example, fruit, vegetable, fish or chicken. Skinning is undertaken for a variety of reasons including to improve appearance and taste, and for health and safety reasons. Note that 'peeling' and 'skinning' are interchangeable terms. Peeling is normally used when referring to fruit and vegetables, and skinning when referring to animals.

Equipment required

The equipment required for skinning will vary according to the type of item to be skinned. Typical equipment includes vegetable knife, vegetable peeler, filleting knife and cook's knife.

Hints and tips

Chicken is a healthy food. However, by removing the skin of the chicken before eating, you can reduce the fat content by half. Leaving the skin on during cooking generally prevents the meat from drying out, leaving the flesh more tender and moist, but remember to remove the skin before serving if you want to reduce the fat content.

For you to do

11 Make a list of three foods that you would skin using each of these items of equipment:

    a filleting knife

    b vegetable peeler.

Strain

Description

Straining is the process of separating liquid from a solid food by passing through a strainer or sieve.

Equipment required

There are many different types of strainers that can be used to strain different types of foods.

■ A steel funnel with strainer is useful for removing food **debris** from cooking oil.

■ A basket strainer is useful for scooping solid cooked foods out of hot fat, water or stock.

■ A chinois (left) is a **conical** sieve used to strain stock and sauces, or crush soft, cooked foods such as tomatoes and apples into thick purées.

Hints and tips

When a clear liquid is required, for example in jam making, professional cooks sometimes use a straining bag made from **muslin** or use a layer of muslin in a conical strainer. Muslin helps to remove any fine **sediment** so leaving the liquid very clear.

Conical: *shaped like a cone.*
Debris: *small particles or bits of food broken up during cooking, for example, crumbs.*
Muslin: *very fine, thin cotton material.*
Sediment: *soft substance that is like a wet powder, made of fine particles of solid food ingredients that settle at the bottom of the cooking liquid.*

Culinary Terms

There are a number of culinary terms that are used in professional kitchens, throughout the world. Most of these terms are in French and are derived from French cookery. There are five particular culinary terms that you will have to know and also practise.

Term		Definition
Macedoine		Cutting of vegetables into small cubed dice, usually 5mm x 5mm x 5mm in size.
Jardinière		Cutting of vegetables into batons, usually 3mm x 3mm x 18mm in size.
Julienne		Cutting into long, thin, matchstick-sized strips, usually 20 mm in length and 1mm in thickness.
Paysanne		Cutting of vegetables into thin slices of 1cm diameter or side according to shape. Normally triangles, squares or rounds are cut, depending on the vegetable being used.
Brunoise		Cutting of vegetables into very small dice. If used for a soup, size would normally be 2mm x 2mm x 2mm, but for a garnish would be smaller – 1mm x 1mm x 1mm.

For you to do

12 Find out the meaning of each of the following terms:
  a mirepoix
  b concassé
  c à la mode
  d au jus
  e entrée
  f sabayon.

Presentation and Garnishes

Even the most plain and simple food can look attractive and appetising when presentation techniques are used effectively. Presentation (or the assembly of food onto the plate) is helped by using appropriate garnishing or decoration techniques.

Remember, garnishes are usually edible decorations added to savoury dishes, whereas decorations are usually edible items added to sweet dishes.

There are a number of reasons why we decorate or garnish foods:

- to improve the overall look of the food being served
- to indicate portioning of food
- to add flavour and texture to food, as garnishes and decorations are generally edible.

It is important that food is not over-decorated or over-garnished. Any garnish or decoration should complement the flavour, colour, texture, size and taste of the food being served.

There are a number of different rules that should be followed when garnishing or decorating.

Rule 1 Use Correct Equipment

Just as it is important to use the correct equipment for different food preparation tasks, so you should use the correct equipment when decorating or garnishing. Some of the equipment used in garnishing and decorating is specialist, but some of it is quite standard.

Apple corer

An apple corer can be used to cut small thin rounds from hard fruits and vegetables, for example, apples and carrots.

Melon baller

A melon baller (left) is used to create small balls of fruits or vegetables, for example, melon, cucumber and apple. The baller has a small hole at the base for the easy release of the prepared ball. A melon baller can be bought in different sizes to give different ball sizes.

Zester

A zester (left) is used to remove thin, even strips from the skin or flesh of fruits and vegetables, particularly citrus fruits. The strips can be used as a garnish or decoration. The zester can also be used to create a zig-zag edge to slices of a fruit or vegetable, for example, cucumber.

Butter curler

A butter curler (right) is used to shape butter into delicate butter curls. This helps with the portioning of butter at meals. For easiest use, the butter should be hard and the curler immersed in hot water immediately prior to shaping.

Julienne peeler

A julienne peeler is used to cut vegetables into thin, even-sided batons or strips. This works in a similar way to a potato peeler, but the blades are specially shaped to provide 'julienne' vegetables.

For you to do

13 Visit the Chef Harvey website.

Look at each of the following specialist tools that can be used for decorating or garnishing:

a carrot curler

b 6-piece stainless steel garnishing carving set.

c vegetable cutters set

For each tool write a short description of how it is used.

14 Look at the 'Applebird' graphic on the home page of Chef Harvey. This attractive decoration was made from a red apple using only a sharp vegetable knife! Use one of the links and watch how to make the decoration. Practise making the applebird, but remember that the smaller the apple, the smaller the finished item of decoration.

Links to these sites and other websites relating to Intermediate 2 Hospitality can be found at: www.leckieandleckie.co.uk by clicking on the Learning Lab button and navigating to the Intermediate 2 Hospitality Course Notes page.

Rule 2 Use Garnishes or Decorations to Indicate Portion Size

As well as being used to improve the appearance of foods, garnishes and decorations can be used to help with the portioning of foods.

Pecan nuts have been used in this cheesecake as a decoration (top left). There are a total of 16 pecan nuts arranged around the outside edge of the cheesecake. This cheesecake would serve eight people, so when cutting up the cheesecake you would allow two pecan nuts per slice.

Pepperoni has been used to garnish this pizza (bottom left). There are a total of 12 pepperoni slices arranged around the outside edge of the pizza. This pizza would serve four people, so when cutting up the pizza you would allow three pepperoni slices per person.

Rule 3 Try to Use Fresh Garnishes

Ideally, garnishes and decorations should be edible. For this reason it is important that all decorations and garnishes are as fresh as possible.

Rule 4 Use Decorations and Garnishes That Are in Proportion to the Food Being Served.

It is important that garnishes and decorations are in proportion to the size of the food being served. A simple common garnish is a wedge of lemon. A large wedge of lemon might be appropriate to accompany a main course fish dish, but would be too big for a cheesecake or small fairy cakes.

For you to do

15 Make a list of three different types of food that you would decorate or garnish with a wedge of lemon.

Simple Decorations and Garnishes to Practise

Segmenting an orange

Separating an orange into its individual segments is a common and simple garnish/decoration. For a more delicate decoration, sometimes you also need to remove the skin and inner membranes. As explained earlier, this is often still called segmenting, although its proper name is 'to supreme' the fruit.

Start by removing a slice from the top and bottom of the orange. This provides a steady base from which you can start the process of removing the outer skin.

Cut the outer skin from the flesh starting at the top and moving to the bottom. You need to follow the natural shape of the orange to remove the outer skin and pith but not any excess flesh. This needs lots of practice.

Then remove any remaining pith before cutting into individual segments. You segment the orange by cutting along side each segment membrane to free the flesh.

Hints and tips

Once all of the segments have been removed, squeeze the remaining flesh in the palm of your hands to obtain any remaining orange juice. If you have left some of the flesh on any of the skin, you can squeeze this to make sure that you have removed as much juice as possible.

Using citrus loop

This delicate garnish can be made from orange, lemon or lime, and can be used on water glasses or on the edge of salads.

Wash the fruit and dry it using kitchen paper. Place the fruit on a chopping board and cut a thin slice. Place it flat on to the board and cut it in half, making a half moon shape. Using a small vegetable knife, cut round the fruit where the flesh and the pith meet, but only cut three quarters of the way round the piece. Finally, curl the thin slice of fruit skin tucking it up against the part of the peel that remains attached to the citrus fruit slice.

Using parsley

Parsley is a simple but effective garnish. It is a herb which adds both flavour and colour. There are two main ways in which parsley can be used for garnishing:

- chopped parsley
- parsley en branche (a sprig of parsley).

If using chopped parsley, wash the parsley and dry it well using kitchen paper. Place it on a chopping board and chop it finely using a sharp knife.

If using parsley en branche, select a branch or sprig or parsley, again wash and pat it dry using kitchen paper. Place it on to the food being garnished. Remember that the size of the branch or sprig of parsley should be in proportion to the size of the food being garnished.

Using chocolate

Chocolate can be used as decoration for many sweet items. It can be finely grated and sprinkled over foods to provide colour, or melted and used in many different ways to provide swirls, drizzles, curls and even petal and flower effects.

To make chocolate curls, use a vegetable peeler with a long narrow blade and a thick bar of chocolate. Warm the peeler blade and the chocolate slightly. Make sure that the peeler is completely dry, then use the peeler to peel along the smooth surface of the chocolate, creating chocolate curls.

To make grated chocolate, use a block of chocolate that is cool and firm and then grate using a hand grater. The larger the grater holes, the larger the chocolate grate will be. Remember to clean the grater surface regularly otherwise the chocolate will not grate well.

For you to do

16 Visit the Chocolate Source website. Find and write down the instructions for making chocolate leaves and chocolate shells.

Links to this site and other websites relating to Intermediate 2 Hospitality can be found at: www.leckieandleckie.co.uk by clicking on the Learning Lab button and navigating to the Intermediate 2 Hospitality Course Notes page.

LECKIE-&LECKIE
Learning Lab

Using icing sugar and cocoa powder

Not all decorations and garnishes need to be complex. Icing sugar and/or cocoa powder can be lightly sprinkled over items such as cakes to provide an attractive finish.

Start by sieving the icing sugar or cocoa powder to remove lumps. Then, using a fine sieve, gently dust the top of the item to be decorated.

Ingredients for Healthy Eating

The hospitality industry (restaurants, pubs, cafés, hotels) has an important role to play in promoting healthy eating. Eating outside the home is commonplace. A recent study showed that 97% of people who eat in pubs and restaurants think that the customer has the right to choose a healthy meal.

2 *Food News*

Top chef Jamie Oliver launched a high profile campaign to try to improve the health standard of school dinners across the UK.

In Scotland the Scottish Government has introduced free school meals for some primary school children in order to encourage a healthy and nutritious diet. The Scottish Government has also provided guidelines in relation to the minimum nutritional standards of school meals. However, other parts of the hospitality industry are not required to meet such minimum standards.

However, the Scottish Government has produced a list of guidelines that everybody should follow in order to achieve a healthy **balanced diet**. These are part of the Government's Scottish Diet Action Plan. The following advice relates to the Action Plan's recommendations.

How can the caterer try to ensure that they produce healthy food? There are four main aspects of cooking that promote healthy eating:

- knowledge of healthy eating
- selecting the right ingredients
- selecting the right methods of food preparation
- selecting the right cooking methods.

Knowledge of Healthy Eating: The Eatwell Plate

If you ask a group of people what they think 'healthier catering and eating' means, you would probably get a range of statements.

Healthy catering is:

- about taking chips off the menu
- offering a vegetarian option on a menu
- using brown rice and wholemeal pasta with everything
- highlighting a 'healthy' item on the menu.

In fact, healthy eating and catering is none of these. A healthy diet:

- has plenty of fruit
- has plenty of vegetables
- has plenty of in cereals
- is low in fat
- is low in sugar
- is low in salt.

A healthy diet is also about:

- eating the right foods according to your activity levels
- eating a range of foods to make sure that you are getting a balanced diet.

The **Eatwell plate** is designed by the UK government to give guidance on how to obtain a balanced diet, as illustrated below.

The different-sized sections of the plate show that there are some foods that you should eat more of, such as fruit and vegetables, and bread, rice, potatoes and pasta, and that there are some foods and drinks you should consume less of, such as those which are high in fat and/or sugar.

The Eatwell plate is based on five food groups:

- bread, rice, potatoes and pasta
- fruit and vegetables
- meat, fish, eggs and beans
- milk and dairy foods
- foods and drinks containing a high amount of fats and sugar.

To ensure a balanced healthy diet you should consume foods from the first four groups every day. Choosing different foods from within each section is also encouraged, as variety promotes balance within the diet. The items in the last group are not essential to a healthy diet, but do provide some variety. The Eatwell model doesn't mean that you shouldn't choose foods and drinks containing fats and sugar, just that you should limit your intake.

Let's look at each of the food groups in more detail and see how we can incorporate these foods into a healthy diet

Bread, Rice, Potatoes and Pasta

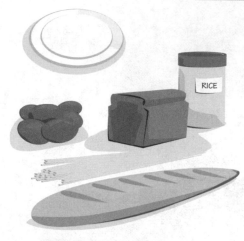

Bread, rice, potatoes and pasta are starchy foods which are high in carbohydrate, low in fat and provide many important vitamins and minerals and are filling. Wholegrain and wholemeal varieties of breads, rice and pasta provide fibre.

These foods should form the basis of each meal and the caterer should offer at least two servings of **cereals**, breads, potatoes, pasta or rice at each meal.

One serving is equivalent to:

- one bowl of breakfast cereal, preferably not sugar-coated varieties
- one slice of bread, preferably wholemeal or wholegrain
- one medium potato, but not in the (high fat) form of chips or roasted potatoes
- one dessertspoon of cooked pasta or rice, ideally wholemeal.

> **Cereal:** *a grass such as rice or wheat that produces grains or seeds which can be used as a food source.*

The following ideas show ways of increasing intake of bread, cereals, potatoes, pasta and rice.

- Breakfast cereals should be high in **fibre** and low in sugar, and should be served daily.
- Potatoes should be boiled or baked and can be served plain, or mashed. These should be served daily. Avoid serving chips or roasted potatoes as these have a higher fat content than other options.
- If serving mashed potatoes, use skimmed milk and low-fat spread rather than full-cream milk and butter.
- If roasted potatoes or chips are on the menu, then healthier alternatives such as boiled or baked potatoes should also be available.
- Different types of breads, for example, wholemeal bread, crusty baguettes, brown rolls and pitta breads, should be available on the menu.
- When cooking use wholemeal flour rather than refined white flour, especially in baked products.
- If serving biscuits, they should be plain and made of wholemeal flour rather than sweet, chocolate covered and made of white flour.
- If making fruit crumble, use porridge oats as a topping as an alternative to the traditional fat/flour crumble topping.

Fruit and Vegetables

> **Anti-oxidant:** *a substance which slows down the rate at which something suffers damage.*

Fruit and vegetables are important sources of vitamins and minerals, especially Vitamins A, C, E and B complex, including folic acid. Vitamins A, C and E are known as **anti-oxidant** vitamins and it is thought these may help protect against heart disease and some cancers. Fruit and vegetables are also low in calories and almost all are fat free.

The caterer should offer at least one variety of fruit at each meal and at least one portion of vegetables at all midday and evening meals.

One serving is equivalent to:

- half a glass of fruit juice, preferably unsweetened
- three dessertspoons of cooked vegetables or salad
- one small bowl of home-made vegetable soup
- one medium-sized piece of fresh fruit, for example, apple or pear
- three dessertspoons of cooked or tinned fruit, which should be in natural or unsweetened juice.

The following ideas show ways of increasing intake of fruit and vegetables.

- Offer fruit juice at breakfast and at other meals, particularly as a replacement for sweetened carbonated (fizzy) drinks
- Offer two vegetables or a side salad at each meal, as well as a serving of potatoes (see above).
- Vegetables can be used from fresh or frozen state; both are equally nutritious.
- When offering salads, serve them plain and give the customer the option of adding a dressing.
- Salad dressings should be low in fat and low in calories.
- Fruit can be served in a number of ways: fresh, tinned, frozen, cooked, or as a fruit smoothie. Tinned fruit should be unsweetened or tinned in natural fruit juice.
- Home-made vegetable soups are a good way to introduce vegetables into the menu.
- Fresh fruit should always be offered as a dessert choice. Dried fruits can also be offered (but watch portions, as dried fruits are often relatively high in calories).
- Add dried fruits to baked items such as wholemeal scones and biscuits, or to other desserts such as rice puddings.
- Fruit crumbles are a good way of increasing fruit consumption.

Meat, Fish, Eggs and Beans

Meat, fish, eggs and beans are a good source of protein, iron, Vitamin B complex and zinc. However, they can contain moderate amounts of fat.

The caterer should offer red meat a maximum of three times per week. Fish should be offered at least twice a week. On average two servings for this group should be served daily.

One serving of this group is equivalent to:
- 60g cooked lean meat or poultry
- 90g cooked fish
- 2 eggs
- 90g nuts.

The following ideas show ways of increasing intake of meat, fish, eggs, beans and alternatives.

> **Pulses:** *seeds such as beans, peas and lentils which can be cooked and eaten.*

- Add **pulses** such as beans and lentils to meat dishes to increase the fibre content, reduce the total fat content and add extra protein.
- Use plant-based alternatives to meat, such as mycoprotein (Quorn®), tofu, texturised vegetable protein-based products and soya. These products are available in different ways – minced, cubed, dried – suitable for a variety of dishes. They are generally low in fat and high in fibre, so are healthy options for everyone, not just **vegetarians**.
- Serve slightly less meat but provide extra vegetables or starchy foods (e.g. bread, rice, pasta) to maintain meal size.
- Use **lean** cuts of meat or trim the excess fat from meat.
- Remove the skin from poultry before serving.
- Use cooking methods which reduce fat content, for example, grilling.
- Include more fish on the menu, particularly oil-rich fish. White fish contains very little fat so is a healthy choice, but do not coat the fish with batter or creamy sauces.

Milk and Dairy Foods

Milk and dairy foods are an important source of the following nutrients: calcium, protein, Vitamin B_{12} and Vitamins A and D. However, they can have a high fat content so you should try not to serve them too often and/or use low- or reduced-fat versions where possible (and keep portions small).

One serving is equivalent to:
- 200ml milk
- 125ml yoghurt
- 30g cheese.

The following ideas show ways of making the best choices in this food group.
- Use semi-skimmed and skimmed milk as an alternative to full-cream milk.
- Try to buy low-fat versions of dairy products, for example, low-fat cheese or low-fat yoghurt.
- If using cheese, try Edam cheese which is a low-fat cheese.
- Offer semi-skimmed or skimmed milk with tea and coffee.

Foods and Drinks Containing Fat and Sugar

Fat

A small amount of fat is essential for health and it makes food more appetising. Fat actually adds flavour to many foods. However, many people consume more fat than their bodies need for good health. When this happens, they are at greater risk of being overweight or even becoming obese, and they have a higher risk of developing heart disease and other diseases.

Fromage frais: *a type of soft cheese which is low in fat and is often produced with fruit flavours. It is sometimes used as an alternative to yoghurt or cream in recipes.*

Mono-unsaturated fat: *a type of fat or oil which is regarded as less harmful to the body than other types of fat or oil.*

Obese: *be extremely (unhealthily) fat.*

Poly-unsaturated fat: *a type of fat or oil which is regarded as less harmful to the body than other types of fat or oil.*

The following ideas show ways of making the best choices in this food group.

- Use low-fat spreads rather than butter or margarine as this can help to reduce overall fat content.
- **Mono-unsaturated** or **poly-unsaturated** low-fat spreads are better than margarines, but should still be used sparingly.
- Offer pre-packed and pre-portioned low-fat spread or margarine portions to control the amount of fat being served.
- If possible, oven bake or grill foods rather than fry them in order to reduce fat intake.
- Use poly-unsaturated or mono-unsaturated vegetable oils rather than other oils.
- When using meats and meat products, select lean meat and/or remove visible fat.
- Buy meat products with a low fat content. Remember, pies and other processed foods may be high in fat, sugar and salt.
- Choose cooking methods which do not add fat during the cooking process or which remove fat during cooking, for example, grilling.
- Fish and poultry are low in fat, so these should be offered daily on a menu.
- Limit pies and processed meat products to once per week.
- Drain the fat off foods which are baked, fried or deep-fat-fried using kitchen paper in order to soak up any excess fat or oil.
- Use skimmed or semi-skimmed milk rather than full-cream milk when cooking.
- Instead of cream, use low-fat yoghurt, low-fat **fromage frais** or custard made from low-fat milk.

Sugar

Foods containing sugar and sugary drinks provide calories but very few nutrients. Sugary snacks and drinks taken regularly throughout the day are a major cause of tooth decay.

The following ideas show ways of reducing sugar intake.

- Serve good quality fresh fruit as an alternative to or alongside other desserts.
- Avoid serving sweetened breakfast cereals (those coated in sugar or honey).
- Serve unsweetened fruit juices or water and sugar-free drinks (preferably non-carbonated) instead of drinks containing sugar.
- Serve sweets, biscuits and confectionery foods only occasionally. When they are served, they should be plain and wholemeal, such as digestive biscuits.
- Provide sugar alternatives such as artificial sweeteners when serving tea and coffee.
- If possible replace sugar with artificial sweeteners when cooking, for example, when stewing fruit.
- Serve reduced-sugar versions of jams and marmalades as accompaniments to toast, scones, etc.

Hints and tips

Always read food labels carefully. A product advertised as low in fat may seem a healthy choice – but it may actually be high in sugar, and not so healthy after all!

Salt

Although salt is not identified on the Eatwell plate, we need to limit our intake of salt, and foods which have a high salt content. Salt is often added to foods to add or enhance flavour, but there are healthier ways of adding flavour to foods, such as using herbs and spices. A diet high in salt (whether by adding salt to food or consuming salty foods) can contribute to raised blood pressure and to heart disease.

The following ideas show ways of reducing salt intake.

- Use a variety of seasonings such as herbs and spices to flavour foods instead of using salt.
- Do not add salt to food when cooking unless you have tested the food for seasoning.
- Some products, such as soy sauce, have a high salt content and so should not be used often.
- Prepared products, such as dried soups and sauces, can be high in salt so try to use fresh alternatives.
- Buy low-salt versions of snack foods such as popcorn and nuts.

For you to do

1 Read the 'Eatwell plate' booklet provided by your teacher or find it on the Eatwell website and print it out. Then answer these questions.

   a What is meant by 'starchy food'?

   b Should we include frozen and tinned fruits in our selection of fruits and vegetables?

   c To which sections of the Eatwell plate do the following foods belong: butter; eggs; yoghurt?

   d What are 'pulses'?

   e How much oily fish should we eat each week?

   f Give one example of an oily fish.

   g How much is one portion of these foods: fruit juice; salad; grapes?

   h How can we reduce the amount of fat when cooking poultry?

   i Why should we avoid consuming sugary drinks?

Links to the Eatwell website and other websites relating to Intermediate 2 Hospitality can be found at:
www.leckieandleckie.co.uk by clicking on the Learning Lab button and navigating to the Intermediate 2 Hospitality Course Notes page.

Selecting Ingredients for Healthy Eating

The previous section gave many practical examples of how to use knowledge in order to make healthy food choices. The next step for the caterer in promoting a healthy diet is to use their knowledge of healthy eating and choose appropriate ingredients. The following example illustrates how the caterer can do this.

Vegetable soup is traditionally made using these ingredients:

Bouquet garni: *small bunch of dried herbs often wrapped in thin fabric and placed in stews and soups while cooking to add flavour.*
Croûton: *a small cube of bread that is fried or toasted and added to soup or salad just before serving.*

> 1kg mixed vegetables – onion, carrot, turnip, leek and celery
>
> 125g butter
>
> 60g flour
>
> 2.5 litres chicken stock
>
> 300g potatoes
>
> Seasoning – **bouquet garni**, salt, pepper
>
> Serve with **croûtons** – 125g butter, 3 slices white bread

With some minor changes this recipe can be adapted to promote healthy eating. Look at the revised list, with changes highlighted in blue:

> 1kg mixed vegetables – onion, carrot, turnip, leek and celery
>
> 100ml sunflower oil or olive oil
>
> 60g flour
>
> 2.5 litres vegetable stock
>
> 300g potatoes
>
> Seasoning – bouquet garni, reduced/low-salt, pepper
>
> Serve with slices of wholemeal bread

Now look at the notes made by the chef giving reasons for the adaptations:

- Use sunflower or olive oil instead of butter. These contain less saturated fat which is considered bad for our health. The amount of oil has also been reduced.
- Use vegetable stock instead of chicken stock. This may reduce the fat content slightly but will also make this soup suitable for vegetarians.
- Use low-salt* instead of ordinary table salt. An alternative is to use less salt.
  * People with kidney problems might not be able to eat soup made from low-salt alternatives.
- Croûtons are fried, so they increase the fat content of the dish. Instead, serve wholemeal bread (higher fibre content than white bread), along with portions of

Remember that when undertaking this activity, we are trying to adapt the ingredients and not change the recipe completely.

For you to do

2 Study the list of ingredients for making lasagne. Suggest ways of adapting the list to promote healthy eating.

Ingredients for traditional lasagne recipe

Serves 10

300g lasagne sheets

3 tablespoons (33g) oil

250g onion

125g carrot

125g celery

500g minced beef

125g streaky bacon

125g tomato purée

1 litre stock (80g butter, 80g white flour, 1330ml stock)

$1\frac{1}{2}$ cloves (4.5g) garlic

250g mushrooms

sauce (600ml whole milk, 50g white flour, 50g butter)

125g cheddar cheese

seasoning – marjoram, salt, pepper

Preparation Techniques for Healthy Eating

Once the caterer has selected ingredients appropriately, the next step in promoting healthy eating is to use healthy food preparation techniques. These techniques are straightforward and simple – they are designed to retain nutrients within the food and to contribute to a healthy diet, which is:

- high in fruit, vegetables and cereals
- low in fat, sugar and salt.

The following advice shows how food preparation techniques can be used to meet the requirements of a healthy diet. (The selection of cookery processes to ensure healthy eating is covered on pages 41–45.)

Fruit and Vegetables

- When peeling fruits and vegetables such as apples and potatoes, use a vegetable peeler to ensure that you are removing only a thin amount of peel. Using a vegetable knife may result in a thicker peel, removing more of the nutrients found in the flesh and also contributing to food waste. Where appropriate, leave skin on, as this will add fibre.
- When using fresh fruit and vegetables, use the freshest items available, as these will contain most nutrients. Store them only for short periods. Note that some frozen vegetables may contain more nutrients that fresh because they are frozen very quickly after picking.
- Never leave vegetables soaking in water for long periods as water-soluble vitamins B complex and C will leach out into the water and be lost.
- Do not cut vegetables into very small pieces; a greater number of smaller pieces have a greater surface area overall, which means more vitamins can be lost when exposed to air.
- Prepare fruits and vegetables using sharp knives. Blunt knives can bruise the flesh and reduce nutrient content.
- Prepare fruits and vegetables just before they are needed because nutrients are lost during holding.

Hints and tips

Hygiene and food safety tip

! Fresh fruits and some vegetables, for example, peppers, tomatoes and courgettes, should be washed before use. This removes any traces of chemicals such as pesticides, as well as other contaminants. Think about all the people – from farmer to packer to supermarket staff – who may have handled an apple before you buy it. Do you want to take the risk of serving unwashed fruits and vegetables to your friends, family or customers?

Bread, Rice, Potatoes and Pasta

- If your recipe asks you to sieve flour and you are using wholemeal flour, you need to empty the contents of the sieve into the bowl when sifting is finished, otherwise all of the healthy parts of the flour will be left in the sieve.

Meat, Fish, Eggs and Beans

- Remove visible fat from meat to reduce fat content.
- Skim fat from stock, sauces and soups during cooking.
- Drain surface fat from food before serving, for example, by placing the food on absorbent paper before serving.
- Plan menus which keep dishes high in fat to a minimum.
- Vegetarian products such as Tofu, soya and other meat alternatives can be substituted for meat, fish or poultry, particularly when other strongly flavoured ingredients are used.

Milk and Dairy Foods

- Use mature or stronger flavoured cheese so that you can reduce the quantity of cheese in recipes.
- Instead of full-fat cream, use low-fat cream, or reduced-fat yoghurt or crème fraiche, to reduce total fat content.

Foods and Drinks Containing Fat and Sugar

- Thicken mixtures using puréed vegetables instead of the usual flour/butter method.
- When frying food make sure the fat is at the correct temperature as this reduces fat absorption.
- Use non-stick frying pans which require much less fat during cooking.
- To reduce sugar content, use dried fruits instead of sugar in baked goods, for example.

Fact or fiction?

- **One quarter** of teenagers are obese.
- Children with fat parents are **twice** as likely to become obese.
- Kids who are obese in their early teens are **twice** as likely to die by the age of 50.
- Kids eat **40%** more salt that they should.
- **10%** of children do not eat breakfast.
- The average school student spends **£1.75** per day on snacks: 70% buy fizzy drinks, 60% buy drinks and 50% buy chocolate.

Source: www.jamieoliver.com

All of this is true! This is why it is so important that caterers adopt healthy eating guidelines.

For you to do

3 There are specific nutritional guidelines in Scotland for all school meals. The guidelines are designed to promote healthy, nutritional meals. Some of the guidelines are shown below. Study them and provide an explanation for each one.

a Milk
Plain or flavoured drinking milk should be available as an option every day. Semi-skimmed and skimmed milks have the same amount of calcium as whole milk and should be provided for drinking as well as for cooking.

b Fish
Fish, in addition to tuna fish, should appear on the menu a minimum of once a week. Oil-rich fish (sardines, kippers, salmon, mackerel, herring, sild) should be served once a week. Mackerel salads and **pâtés** are often popular.

c Fats
Only poly-unsaturated and mono-unsaturated fats, spreads and oils and low-fat spreads should be used.

Other Issues Affecting Selection of Healthy Ingredients

Vending machines

Many places of employment, schools, colleges and universities have vending machines. Traditionally, these have been stocked with chocolate bars, crisps and sugary drinks. However, they can stock healthier options, such as fresh fruit, yoghurts, brown rolls/sandwiches, cereal bars, plain biscuits, pure fruit juices and water. Provision should be made for regular stocking of fresh items and drinking water facilities should available throughout the workplace or establishment.

The eating environment

It is important to try to encourage people into canteens where healthy food is served. The eating environment should:

- be clean and pleasant, encouraging people to use the facilities
- have food storage and heating facilities for those workers who take in their own food
- prominently display information and advice about healthy eating.

The use of organic food

Organic food is produced naturally without the use of artificial chemicals such as insecticides and chemical fertilisers.

People buy organic foods believing that organic foods are healthier because they have not been subjected to chemical or artificial treatments. There are also claims that organic foods are more nutritious but these claims have not been proven.

The Soil Association is a UK body that sets out rules and regulations for farmers who wish to grow and sell organic foods. These rules and regulations are designed to prevent producers from labelling and selling their produce as 'organic' when in fact it is not organic, so protecting the public from misleading claims.

For you to do

4 Visit the vending machine in your school and make a list of the types of products it provides. What can you conclude about the promotion of health in your school through the use of vending machines?

5 Write a short paragraph about the eating environment in your school canteen. Do you think that this environment encourages people to use the canteen? What steps could be made to improve the situation?

6 Visit the website of the Soil Association. Make a list of products that can be organic. Draw the Soil Association Organic Symbol.

Cookery Processes for Healthy Eating

Just as it is important to select the correct ingredients for a healthy diet and then prepare these to meet healthy eating guidelines, so the methods of cooking food also affect how healthy the food will be.

Methods of cookery are generally classified as being **wet** or **dry**.

- Wet methods of cooking involve cooking food in a liquid. Wet methods include: boiling, steaming, poaching and stewing, braising and pot roasting.
- Dry methods of cooking do not require the use of a liquid. Dry methods include: grilling, baking, roasting, stir-frying and microwave cooking.

Note: It might seem that stir-frying should be classified as a wet method of cooking. However, frying is classified as a dry method because the food is submerged or placed in fat that does not contain water.

The main methods of cookery that promote healthy eating are described below. These are the best cookery methods for retaining both flavour and nutrients in food without adding excessive amounts of fat, salt or sugar.

Dry Methods of Cooking

Baking

Baking is often associated with breads, pastries and biscuits, but you can also bake seafood, poultry, lean meat, and similarly-sized pieces of vegetables and fruit. In this dry method of cooking, food is placed in a pan or dish surrounded by the hot, dry air of an oven. The food can be cooked covered or uncovered.

How does baking contribute to healthy eating?

- No additional fat is required for foods such as baked potatoes or apples.
- Nutrition loss is minimal.

Example: a baked apple stuffed with dried fruits.

Grilling

In this dry method of cooking, thin pieces of food are placed under direct heat to enable cooking. Foods suitable for grilling include fish, meat and meat dishes such as steak and burgers, and vegetables.

How does grilling contribute to healthy eating?

- Grilling allows fat to drip away from the food, reducing fat content.
- Lean or trimmed meat can be used, which reduces fat content further.
- No additional fat is required for cooking (some may be used to brush foods before grilling to prevent the food from drying out, but this would involve only a minimal amount of oil).

Example: grilled sirloin steak.

Microwaving

Microwave cookery is a dry method of cookery where food is cooked by microwave rays (these are high frequency electromagnetic waves). The microwaves penetrate the food from different directions causing it to heat up – and cook – from the inside to the outside. Most foods can be microwaved, but because there is no direct heat source, products will not brown and pastry products will not crisp up. You cannot shallow-fry or deep-fry using a microwave cooker.

How does microwaving contribute to healthy eating?

- Little or no fat needs to be added.
- Little water is needed for cooking, so nutrient loss is minimal.
- The cooking process is very quick, so nutrient loss is minimal

Example: microwaved baked apple.

Roasting

Roasting is a dry method of cooking similar to baking, but usually at higher temperatures. Like baking, roasting uses an oven's dry heat to cook the food. Suitable foods include meat, vegetables such as potatoes, poultry and game.

How does roasting contribute to healthy eating?

- Poultry, seafood and meat can be placed on a rack inside the roasting pan so that fat can drip away from the food during cooking.
- Little or no fat needs to be added.
- Nutrient loss can be minimal.

Example: roast vegetables.

Pot roasting

Baste: *to spoon cooking juices over meat as it cooks, adding flavour and retaining moisture.*

Pot roasting is a dry method of cooking and is similar to roasting because it involves cooking meat and poultry in the oven where the food can be **basted** with fat, if required. Traditionally, pot roasting should be carried out in a heavy pot with a tight-fitting lid. The food is cooked on a bed of vegetables in the pot. The pot roast can also be cooked over a flame on the hob. This is a slow method of cooking and is best used for less expensive, tougher cuts of meat.

How does pot roasting contribute to healthy eating?

- Little or no fat is added.
- There will be some nutrient loss with this process, but in some cases the cooking liquid can be kept and used for making stock or soup.
- Vegetables are included in the dish.

Example: pot roasted fillet of beef.

Stir-frying

This is classified as a dry method of cooking as only a very small amount of oil is required. Stir-frying originates from Asia, and involves quickly stirring small, evenly-sized pieces of food in a wok or large non-stick frying pan. Suitable foods include small strips of meat, fish, poultry, vegetables, rice and noodles.

How does stir-frying contribute to healthy eating?

- You need only a small amount of oil or non-stick cooking spray for this cooking method.
- Because the cooking process is so quick, most nutrients are retained.

Example: stir-fried chicken with noodles.

Wet Methods

Boiling

Boiling is a wet method of cooking in which prepared food is cooked in a liquid such as water or stock. Boiling can be a quick and rapid process used for cooking vegetables such as potatoes, or it can be a longer, slower process known as **simmering**. Suitable foods include meat, poultry, shellfish, eggs, pasta, rice and vegetables.

How does boiling contribute to healthy eating?

- No fat is added.
- Boiling may result in some nutrient loss, but in some cases the cooking liquid can be kept and used for making stock or soup.

Example: boiled potatoes.

Braising

Braising is a wet method of cooking where prepared food is cooked in the oven in a covered container with an amount of stock or liquid. Braised food is normally placed on a bed of vegetables and then liquid is added (covering about two thirds of the food being braised). Suitable foods include meat, poultry, vegetables and rice.

How does braising contribute to healthy eating?

- Little or no fat needs to be added.
- There will be some nutrient loss, but in some cases the cooking liquid is served as a gravy or sauce.
- Vegetables are included in the dish.

Example: braised shoulder steak.

Poaching

Poaching is a wet method of cooking where foods such as eggs, fruits, fish and poultry are gently simmered in water, stock, vinegar or juice until they're cooked through and tender. This is a gentle process, so poached foods retain their shape during cooking.

How does poaching contribute to healthy eating?

- Generally, no additional fat is required.
- Only a small amount of liquid needs to be used and so nutrient loss is minimal.

Example: poached pears.

Steaming

Steaming is a wet method of cooking, and uses water vapour (steam) to cook the food. It usually involves holding the food over simmering water so that the steam generated circulates around the food and cooks it. You can also buy electric steamers which make steaming even easier. Suitable foods include fish, meat, vegetables, rice and puddings, for example, steamed sponge.

How does steaming contribute to healthy eating?

- No fat is required.
- Nutrient loss is minimal as food does not come into direct contact with cooking liquid.
- Steaming retains the flavour of vegetables, so salt doesn't need to be added.

Example: steamed rice.

Stewing

This wet method of cooking can be used with many different ingredients ranging from meat and poultry to fruit and vegetables. Stewing involves slowly and gently cooking the food in a pan on top of the hob with a small quantity of liquid, such as water or stock. In some recipes, the cooking liquid is used as the base for a sauce that is served with the dish, such as in a beef stew. A complete meal can be made in one container using healthy ingredients.

How does stewing contribute to healthy eating?

- No additional fat is required.
- Nutrient loss is minimal as any nutrients that seep into the cooking liquid can be saved if the cooking liquid is served with the stewed dish.
- Lean or trimmed meat can be used, reducing the fat content.

Example: beef and vegetable stew.

Hints and tips

Healthy eating tip: Using herbs and spices

✔ Using herbs and spices is a great way to add flavour to food and reduce the amount of salt used when cooking. If using fresh herbs make sure they are freshly picked. Why not grow some in pots on the kitchen windowsill? Dried herbs are a convenient alternative but they are stronger in flavour than fresh herbs, so use only about one third of the amount.

Healthy eating tip: Cooking vegetables

✔ Nutrients are easily lost when cooking vegetables, but there are a number of steps you can take to minimise nutrient loss.

✔ Use only a little water, as you are likely to lose more nutrients if you use more water.

✔ Speed up the cooking process (and minimise nutrient loss) by placing prepared vegetables into boiling water and/or use a covered pan.

✔ Keep the cooking liquid and use it to make stock or soups.

For you to do

7 Using the internet, try to find healthy recipes for each of the following dishes. Print each recipe that you find.

■ Scottish rich beef stew ■ Baked apple

■ Baked cod ■ Steamed pudding

8 Copy and complete the chart below to provide a 'healthy eating' checklist for each different cookery process.

Cookery method	Fat content			Nutrient content	
	Increased	Maintained	Reduced	Maintained	Reduced
Stir-frying	Slightly				
Steaming			in some foods	✔	
Braising					
Boiling					
Stewing					
Poaching					
Baking					
Roasting					
Grilling					

Planning Your Work

Good planning and organisation of your work is the key to being a successful caterer. Effective planning means that you think through all your tasks in advance, to make sure that all ingredients are prepared, cooked and served at the appropriate time.

Part of the planning process involves creating a contingency plan (a 'plan B') for unexpected problems. So planning also helps you to be prepared for things that go wrong or not as planned.

When planning your work there are a number of key terms that you need to be familiar with:

- **task:** a piece of work to be undertaken or completed, for example a recipe
- **component parts:** the ingredients
- **processes:** the steps that have to be undertaken to complete the dish.

Let's look at each of these in more detail, using a specific example – the task of making Special Chicken Chow Mein for four people.

The Task

Your task is to make a Special Chicken Chow Mein that will serve four people.

First, look at the recipe for Special Chicken Chow Mein to identify the component parts and the processes.

Recipe: Special Chicken Chow Mein

Ingredients
350g Chinese egg noodles
30ml oil
100g boneless pork
100g boneless chicken
100g peeled prawns
50g canned water chestnuts
50g spring onions
15ml soy sauce

Serves: 4   Cooking time: 15 minutes

> The ingredients are the component parts. This task has eight component parts.

> Each of the main steps in the method are the processes, for example:
> - *chopping the spring onions finely*
> - *stir-frying until lightly browned.*
> Remember that there can be more than one process in each step of the method.

Method

1 Cook the noodles in plenty of boiling water for 3–5 minutes or until tender.
2 Drain and set aside.
3 Chop the spring onions finely.
4 Prepare the pork and chicken by dicing evenly.
5 Heat the oil in a wok and add the pork and chicken.
6 Stir-fry until lightly browned.
7 Add the prawns and chestnuts and cook for a few minutes.
8 Stir in the cooked noodles and toss with the ingredients until heated through.
9 Add the spring onions and soy sauce.
10 Serve.

Developing a Plan of Work

Now you know the meaning of the terms involved in planning your work, you can look at how to develop a plan of work, using the Special Chicken Chow Mein recipe as an example.

Imagine you have been given 50 minutes to collect all the ingredients and equipment for this recipe, then prepare and serve the Chow Mein. You would need to complete a work plan or time plan sheet similar to the one below. The purpose of the time plan sheet is to allow you to plan and time the sequence of processes that you will have to complete when carrying out this task.

Times are normally allocated in blocks of 5 minutes. You should try to divide your task into easily identified stages. These stages will combine a number of processes.

Remember to wash your hands at the start of the task. Wash them again after handling raw ingredients, such as raw poultry.

This column is useful for making notes such as oven temperatures and the finishing times of cooking processes.

Times	Activities	Notes
10.05 – 10.10	Boil a pan of water. Wash and pat dry the chicken and pork. Dice into bite-sized cubes.	
10.10 –10.15	Chop spring onions finely. Add noodles to water.	Noodles ready at 10.18
10.15 – 10.25	Heat the oil and stir-fry the chicken and pork. Drain noodles.	
10.25 – 10.30	Add the prawns and water chestnuts. Cook for a few minutes.	
10.30 – 10.35	Clean work surface. Stack dishes for washing.	
10.35 – 10.40	Stir in the noodles and heat through.	
10.40 – 10.45	Clean table and wash dishes.	
10.45 – 10.50	Serve.	

It is important to plan time to tidy the work area and for washing dishes during the task.

Hints and tips

Careful and effective planning is always important to the success of a task. It is a good idea to read over all recipes carefully so that you fully understand each part of the recipe. It is also a good idea when you have completed a time plan to run through it before any assessment. That way you can test your time plan to make sure it works.

For you to do

9 Complete a work plan for the dish provided below. You have a total of 60 minutes to prepare, cook and serve the dish, starting at 1 pm and finishing at 2 pm.

Sweet and Sour Chicken

Ingredients

455g skinless, boneless chicken breast meat, cubed

30ml vegetable oil

45g sliced red pepper

1 clove garlic, crushed

60ml soy sauce

15ml vinegar

1.25ml ground ginger

45g sliced green pepper

120g carrot batons

8g corn flour

1 can (200g) pineapple chunks, juice reserved

15g brown sugar

100g rice

Method

1 Prepare the ingredients as indicated in the recipe.

2 **Brown** the chicken in oil in a large pan over medium-high heat.

3 Add green pepper, red pepper, carrot and garlic and stir-fry for 1–2 minutes.

4 In a small bowl, combine corn flour and soy sauce and mix together.

5 Pour mixture into the frying pan along with the pineapple and liquid, vinegar, sugar and ginger. Stir together and bring to boil for a few minutes.

6 Boil the rice in salted water for 15 minutes. Drain the rice.

7 Serve the sweet and sour chicken with the boiled rice.

Hints and tips

Hygiene and food safety tips

! When using raw meat, for example pork and chicken fillets, rinse them in cold water to remove any excess blood and then pat dry using a paper towel. Remember to dispose of the paper towel safely and to wash your hands immediately after.

! When preparing fruits and vegetables, for example spring onions, remember to wash the item first in cold water to remove any chemical residues or other contaminants. Pat dry with a disposable towel before using. Again, remember to dispose of the paper towel safely and to wash your hands.

Costing

So far, the Special Chicken Chow Mein recipe has been used to help you write a time plan. The same recipe is used now to help you to understand what food costing means.

In the hospitality industry it is important to know how much it costs to produce different dishes that appear on a menu. This ensures that items on the menu are priced appropriately. It also helps with budgeting procedures within the restaurant or kitchen.

To begin with, look at the following example of a recipe costing sheet.

RECIPE COSTING SHEET

Dish:..

Portions required: *The number of portions specified in the task.* Recipe portions: *The number of portions specified in the recipe.*

Ingredients	Recipe measures		Actual measures		Costing	
	Units	Millilitres/ Grams	Units	Millilitres/ Grams	Unit/Litre/ kg price	Total cost £ p

The ingredients used in the recipe.

The measurements used in the recipe. This can be in grams, millilitres or units, e.g. $\frac{1}{2}$ can.

The actual measurements you need to serve the required number of portions.

The cost of the food item, e.g. 39p for a 300g can.

The actual cost of the ingredient for the quantity used in the recipe.

The total cost of the recipe to make for 4 portions.

Cost

Cost per portion

The cost per portion. Divide the total cost by the required number of portions.

Before you start costing a recipe, there are a few important points to remember.

1 You need to check how many portions the recipe is for. This recipe is for four portions.

2 You will normally be cooking food which will serve four portions.

3 You need to work out the cost of producing four portions of a recipe, before working out the cost of one portion.

4 In order to get up-to-date prices for food items, try using the internet, for example, the websites of supermarkets. For links to some websites, go to the Learning Lab page on the Leckie and Leckie website.

5 Round prices up when the decimal part of the cost is above 0.5 pence, for example, round 1.67p up to 2p.

6 Round prices down when the decimal part of the cost is below 0.5 pence, for example, round 1.2p down to 1p.

7 There is a basic costing formula to use:

$$\frac{\text{unit cost}}{\text{unit price}} \times \text{quantity required}$$

The following example shows how to work out the cost of making one portion of the Special Chicken Chow Mein recipe.

Recipe: Special Chicken Chow Mein

Ingredients

350g Chinese egg noodles

30ml oil

100g boneless pork

100g boneless chicken

100g peeled prawns

50g canned water chestnuts

50g spring onions

15ml soy sauce

Serves: 4

Now fill in the columns and do all the calculations to work out the total cost. (The calculations are shown in detail on pages 51–52.)

RECIPE COSTING SHEET

Dish: *Special Chicken Chow Mein*

Portions required: *4*   Recipe portions: *4*

Ingredients	Recipe measures		Actual measures		Costing	
	Units	Millilitres/ Grams	Units	Millilitres/ Grams	Unit/Litre/ kg price	Total cost £ p
Chinese egg noodles		350g		350g	99p/375g	0.92
oil		30ml		30ml	63p/100ml	0.19
pork		100g		100g	634p/1000g	0.63
chicken		100g		100g	769p/1000g	0.77
prawns		100g		100g	100p/100g	1.00
canned chestnuts		50g		50g	125p/300g	0.21
spring onions		50g		50g	48p/50g	0.48
soy sauce		15ml		15ml	88p/150ml	0.09
					Cost	4.29
					Cost per portion	1.07

Total cost of 4 portions = £4.29
Total cost of 1 portion = £1.0725
Total cost of portion = £1.07

Calculating ingredient costs in detail

Example
Chinese egg noodles cost 99p for 375g.

To get the cost of 1 gram we divide the cost of the noodles by the weight of the noodles: 99p ÷ 375g = 0.264p/g

This gives a total of 0.26 pence for 1 gram of noodles.

The recipe uses 350 grams of noodles and so we multiply the cost of 1 gram (0.264p) by 350: 0.264p/g x 350g = 92.4p

Since the decimal part is less than 0.5, we round the figure down, to give a total of 92 pence (£0.92).

You should follow this same process to cost all the ingredients in the recipe.

oil	pork
oil costs 63p for 100ml	pork costs 634p for 1000g
1ml costs 63/100 =0.63p	1g costs 634/1000 = 0.634p
30ml costs 0.63 x 30 =18.9p	100g costs 0.634 x 100 = 63.4p
total cost is 19p (£0.19)	*total cost is 63p (£0.63)*
chicken	**prawns**
chicken costs 769p for 1000g	prawns cost 100p for 100g
1g costs 769/1000 = 0.769p	quantity used is 100g
100g costs 0.769 x 100 = 76.9p	*total cost is 100p (£1.00)*
total cost 77p (£0.77)	
tinned chestnuts	**spring onions**
chestnuts cost 125p for 300g can	spring onions cost 48p for 50g bunch
1g costs 125/300 = 0.417p	quantity used is 50g
50g costs 0.417 x 50 = 20.85p	*total cost 48p (£0.48)*
total cost = 21p (£0.21)	
soy sauce	
soy sauce costs 88p for 150ml	
1ml costs 88/150 = 0.59p	
15ml costs 0.59 x 15 =8.85p	
total cost = 9p (£0.09)	

For you to do

10 Look at the ingredients used in a recipe to make a creamy curried pasta. Visit a supermarket website to find out the unit cost of each ingredient and then work out the cost of making one portion of the recipe.

Ingredients

225g pasta shapes	10ml apricot jam
50g onion	10ml lemon juice
60ml sherry	300g sausages
150ml mayonnaise	50g fresh tomato
10ml curry paste	5ml parsley
Serves 4	

Links to supermarket websites and other websites relating to Intermediate 2 Hospitality can be found at: www.leckieandleckie.co.uk by clicking on the Learning Lab button and navigating to the Intermediate 2 Hospitality Course Notes page.

Food Safety

There are about 80 000 reported cases of food poisoning in the UK each year and possibly as many as 2 500 000 unreported cases each year.

Food businesses have a duty and a responsibility to provide food to consumers in a safe and hygienic manner. It is important that all food businesses:

- comply with food safety regulations
- demonstrate how to prepare food safely
- train staff to prepare food safely.

If they do not do these things, and cause consumers to become ill, they risk damaging their reputation and their profit.

This section provides an overview of some of the important aspects of food safety and hygiene procedures that should be followed by people preparing and cooking food for public consumption.

There are two main categories of food hygiene:

- **personal hygiene:** relates to the person undertaking the food preparation or cooking
- **kitchen hygiene:** relates to the food preparation and cooking environment.

Personal Hygiene

There are a number of personal hygiene rules that the food worker should follow when preparing or cooking food to ensure that food is safe to eat.

Rule 1: Clean protective clothing should be worn in food preparation and cooking areas.

- Protective clothing is worn to prevent any contamination from outdoor clothing, as this may contain dirt, dust and bacteria which can be transferred to food preparation surfaces, ingredients and equipment.
- Protective clothing should be kept clean. This means that protective clothing should only be worn in the food preparation or cooking area and must be cleaned regularly (preferably daily).

Rule 2: Hair must be tied back (if long) and covered with a hair net, head scarf or chef's hat.

- Wearing protective headgear can prevent strands of hair or even flakes of skin from the head (dandruff) falling into food that is being prepared or cooked.
- Never, under any circumstances, comb or bush your hair in a food preparation or cooking area.

Rule 3: Hands and nails must be kept clean.

- The hands and nails of the food worker are in constant contact with food and so could spread bacteria very easily. For this reason they must be kept very clean.

- Hands should be washed regularly, and certainly after:
  - visiting the toilet
  - handling raw meat, poultry, fish or root vegetables
  - touching your face or hair
  - blowing your nose.

- Keep fingernails clean; a nailbrush is ideal for this purpose.

- When washing hands and nails, use hand-hot water and soap. It is better to use a disposable towel or a hand-drier than a re-usable towel when drying your hands.

- Do not wear nail varnish when working in a food preparation area as it can flake off and contaminate food.

Rule 4: Cuts, spots, boils and skin infections should be covered.

- Open wounds such as cuts, boils, spots and skin infections are ideal breeding grounds for bacteria. For this reason they should be covered with a waterproof dressing. The dressing should be coloured so that, if it falls off, you can find it easily.

Rule 5: Jewellery should not be worn.

- Jewellery can be a breeding ground for bacteria which can transfer on to food. Stones can fall out of jewellery, again transferring bacteria and also acting as a potential choking hazard.

Rule 6: Health issues must be considered.

- Any form of illness should be reported to a supervisor, particularly if you are suffering from:
  - sickness, for example, cold, flu
  - diarrhoea
  - skin allergies.

Rule 7: No smoking.

- Under no circumstances is smoking permitted in a food preparation or cooking area. Smoking is generally bad for health, but the risk of food contamination from ash or bacteria spreading from lip/mouth is high.

Kitchen Hygiene

There are a number of kitchen hygiene rules that the food worker should follow when preparing or cooking food to ensure that food is safe to eat.

Rule 1: Adopt a 'clean as you go' approach to hygiene.

- Wipe up all spills immediately, as they may attract pests and insects, and also be a safety hazard.

- Clean all work surfaces before and after use, preferably using an anti-bacterial spray.
- Clean all equipment after using it and again before re-using it.

Rule 2: Food preparation areas must be clean and well maintained.

- Toilet facilities should be located well away from food preparation and cooking areas.
- Work surfaces should be easy to clean.
- Lighting should allow good visibility, making cleaning easy and effective.

Rule 3: Food should be covered at all times.

- Cover food to prevent contamination from insects, dust, accidental splashes, etc.

Rule 4: Have separate washing facilities for hands and food.

- All food premises should be designed so that there are separate hand washing and drying facilities for the preparation of food and for personal hygiene. This will reduce the possibility of contamination from hands to food ingredients, work surfaces or equipment.
- It is best to have disposable paper towels or warm air driers for drying hands, as these lessen the chance of contamination from hands to food ingredients, work surfaces or equipment.

Rule 5: All waste should be disposed of correctly.

- Waste bins should be emptied on a regular basis and should have well-fitting lids.
- Effective waste management will reduce the possibility of contamination in the food preparation area as well as making the kitchen environment less attractive to pests.

Rule 6: Animals must not be allowed in food preparation areas

- All animals – whether domestic (pets) or pests (rats, mice, birds, insects) – can carry dangerous bacteria, so they must not be allowed in food preparation or cooking areas.
- Action must be taken to try to prevent animals entering a food preparation area, for example, using electronic fly killers or installing fly screens on windows.
- All infestations of pests must be reported to a supervisor and to local environmental health authorities.

Rule 7: Keep cool food cool; keep hot food hot.

- Food which is to be stored should be kept cool. This means keeping the food at a temperature of below 5°C, which is cool enough to prevent bacteria multiplying.
- Food which is to be reheated for serving should reach a temperature of at least 82°C, which is a hot enough temperature to destroy any dangerous bacteria.
- Food which is being kept warm for serving should be maintained at a temperature of at least 63°C.

For you to do

11 At what temperature should each of the following foods be kept?
Choose from:

- below 5°C
- at least 63°C
- above 82°C

a   A pint of skimmed milk

b   Roast beef on a restaurant carvery

c   A steak pie being sold at a football ground food outlet

d   A fillet of fresh trout

e   Beef stew which is being reheated for lunch

f   A hotdog being served from a fast food outlet

12 Look at the illustration opposite. Spot 10 hygiene rules that are being broken.

China

Background

The People's Republic of China is situated in eastern Asia and has some of its main borders with Mongolia, Russia, Kazakhstan, Nepal, India, Vietnam and North Korea. China is a huge country with a large land area and population. Its population is currently 1.3 billion, making it the most highly populated country in the world.

China is so big in terms of land area that each of its 33 provinces has its own particular agriculture, climate and landscape, which means that the cuisine of each province varies greatly. These differences have resulted in the term 'the Eight Cuisines', describing the great variety in eating habits in different parts of China.

Northern China, stretching from Beijing to Xinjiang, consists of grasslands, mountains and deserts. The climate is severe – cold and dry in winter and hot and dusty in summer. The types of crops grown in this region need to be strong and hardy so they can withstand such climatic variations. Important crops in this area include corn, **sorghum**, wheat, cabbages and root vegetables. Rice is also an important crop in the north but is mainly cultivated in the southern provinces

The bottom half of the country – the provinces surrounding and south of the Yangtze River – has a higher rainfall than the north, but still experiences some extreme temperatures. Rice is the main crop in southern China, but wheat and other grains are also grown.

China has long coast and therefore sea fish plays an important part in Chinese cuisine, particularly in the costal areas. Sea fish of all descriptions are plentiful.

China is a produce-rich country, which means that it produces many food items for both domestic and overseas markets. Northern China grows peaches, apples and melons. Southern China produces **taro root**, **eggplants**, tomatoes and leafy greens, as well as tropical fruits such as **longans**, **litchis**, mangoes, bananas and coconuts.

Chinese Cuisine

Chinese cuisine is not the same as the Chinese food that we eat in Scotland. This type of Chinese food tends to originate from Guangdong (previously known as Canton) and is heavily adapted to meet Scottish taste preferences.

There are many different types of Chinese cooking which vary from province to province, and some of the most popular cuisines are briefly described here.

Cantonese cuisine has many different styles and flavours. Stir-frying is popular in Cantonese cuisine because it is quick, light, and healthy (it uses little fat or oil). Cantonese cuisine is famous for its soups and broths and steamed dumplings. Pork, chicken, seafood and vegetables are the main ingredients used in Cantonese dishes.

Hainanese cuisine is lighter, using milder seasonings. Famous items include noodles and dumplings.

Szechuan food is well known for its strong, powerful flavours which come from the use of many different spices including chillies, garlic, ginger and chilli oil. Popular Szechuan dishes include hot and sour soup and steamed red fish with spicy yellow beans.

A traditional Chinese meal is very different from the Chinese meals that we have in Scotland. A Chinese meal is one in which a whole range of dishes are presented at the table for everyone to share. Unlike in Scotland where rice is served with the main course, rice or another carbohydrate dish such as noodles or a starchy dough-based cake is usually served at the end of the meal indicating that the meal is coming to a close.

Eating in China is also different. A dining table would be set with a bowl (for soup, rice or noodles), chopsticks (for eating), porcelain spoon (for drinking soup), cups for wine or Chinese tea, and a small sauce dish for dipping sauces.

A common utensil in Chinese cooking is the **wok**. This is a special type of deep frying pan, traditionally used for stir-frying. Stir-frying involves quickly moving small, bite-size ingredients in a small amount of oil, and cooking them at a very high temperature, so that the food cooks very quickly.

Stewing is popular in Chinese cookery, where food is slowly simmered in liquid in a closed pot. Food can be stewed whole (for example, fish, including the head and tail), in chunks or in bite-sized bits. In some recipes, such as sharks fin dishes, ingredients are stewed many times.

Boiling involves cooking food in boiling water or stock and this is sometimes called a broth. In Chinese cookery the main ingredients are cooked first, then different items added during the cooking process to add more flavour. The broth can be thickened by using a starch thickener such as corn flour.

Steaming is another popular method of cooking in China. This is usually done in a steamer and just about any kind of food can be cooked in this way. Steamed food is generally moist and tender.

Popular Chinese Dishes

Moon cakes

Moon cakes are sweet pastries containing different fillings but the most popular is lotus paste. The moon cake is the traditional food of the Chinese Moon Festival, which is usually in August each year (it's also known as the Mid-Autumn Festival).

The Moon Festival is as important to Chinese culture and custom as Christmas is in the UK. The Chinese eat the moon cakes at night when the full moon is in the sky.

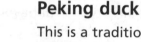

Peking duck

This is a traditional Chinese dish in Beijing (which used to be called Peking). The ducks are raised specifically for human consumption. The ducks are force-fed, kept in cages to stop them from moving about, so they fatten quickly and have a very tender flesh. Steps for roasting the duck are:

- the ducks are rubbed with spices, salt and sugar
- the ducks are hung (stored) in the air for some time
- the ducks are roasted in an oven or hung over the fire until they become brown with rich grease dripping outside and have a nice smell.

Peking duck is always served sliced. Chefs are specially trained in the methods of preparing and serving Peking duck. The whole duck must be sliced into 120 pieces and every piece has to be perfect, with the correct balance between meat and fat. Traditionally Peking duck is served with finely cut onion strips, finely cut cucumber strips, a special dipping sauce and very thin pancakes.

Congee

Congee is a Chinese rice porridge or soup which is generally eaten at breakfast. The rice is cooked in salted water and boiled until it becomes thick and porridge-like. Different ingredients will then be added, such as meat, fish, vegetables, herbs, and nuts, for example, gingko nuts. A sweet congee can be made by adding sugar and Chinese dates called jujubes.

Key Ingredients

Eggplant
The eggplant is a member of the potato family. In the UK it is better known as an aubergine. Eggplants can be cooked in a number of ways: baked, stewed, roasted, grilled and fried.

Litchi
The litchi (or lychee) has been grown in China for hundreds of years. This fruit has a sweet-tart flavour and is often served with duck or pork dishes. A young litchi is pink in colour, which changes to rose and then brown. It has a rough, brittle skin. The clear, jelly-like flesh covers a single seed which is not eaten.

Longan
The longan is a fruit which originates from China and South-East Asia. It resembles the litchi and is often called the litchi's little brother. Its flesh is white and translucent (almost transparent), and it has a grape-like flavour, although it is sweeter than a litchi. Like a litchi it has a small brown seed and is covered with pale brown, brittle skin. The Chinese name means 'dragon's eye'. The fruit is usually just eaten on its own.

Sorghum
Sorghum is a cane-like tropical grass grown for its sweet flavour. It is used to sweeten food, in the production of alcoholic drinks, and also as cattle food.

Taro root
Taro root is a starchy, potato-like vegetable with a brown, hairy skin and grey-white flesh. When cooked, it has a nutty flavour. In China taro roots are often used instead of potatoes. Taro roots can be fried, baked, roasted, boiled or steamed, and are usually served as an accompaniment to meat dishes. They are also used in soups or stews.

Other important ingredients

Celery: often used in stir-fries or served cooked as a vegetable.

Chinese dried black mushrooms: found in most Chinese markets and used in soups and stir-fries.

Chinese rice wine: used to add flavour and is good for removing strong odours, such as fish smells. Chinese rice wine can also be served as a drink in its own right.

Chinese tea: also known as green tea; very popular in China and is usually served at the start of a meal and then throughout the meal. There are many different varieties of Chinese tea.

Corn starch: used to thicken stew and marinades.

Garlic: along with ginger, often used to flavour dishes.

Ginger root: fresh ginger; adds warmth and flavour to dishes.

Ginkgo nut: often used in congee. The ginkgo nut grows on what is believed to be the oldest known living species of tree. It is the seed of an inedible, apricot-like fruit that has a very unusual vomit-like smell.

Green onion: also known as spring onion; often used as a garnish.

Lotus root: the root of a water lily; used as a vegetable. It is crisp when fresh but is also sold dried in many Chinese markets.

Oyster sauce: a thick, dark brown, salty sauce made from oysters.

Rice: long grain rice is used for savoury dishes; short grain or 'sticky' rice is used for desserts or snacks.

Sesame oil: used as a flavouring in stir-fries and soups.

Shallot: related to the onion family but not, as commonly believed, a member of it. Shallots have a mild, slightly sweet taste with a hint of garlic.

Soy sauce: made from the soya bean, and is available in both light and dark versions, the dark being stronger and thicker in texture.

Tofu: also known as soya curd; a soft, cheese-like food made from soy milk, and regarded as a healthy food. Tofu is bland in taste but absorbs the flavours of other ingredients well.

Vegetable oil: generally used in stir-frying.

Do You Know?

4 *Food News*

Chinese government introduces 5% tax on disposable wooden chopsticks in bid to preserve forests

- Many Chinese eating establishments are considering switching from cheap disposable wood chopsticks to more environmentally sustainable and reusable plastic or bamboo chopsticks.
- Traditional Chinese culture considers the use of knives and forks at the table as barbaric because these implements are regarded as weapons.
- Fish are usually cooked and served whole, with diners pulling pieces directly from the fish with chopsticks.
- It is considered bad luck if fish or chicken is served without its head and tail.
- If you order fish in a Chinese restaurant do not be surprised if the waiter comes to the table to show you the live fish. This is to let you know that the fish is fresh!

For you to do

1 Festivals are an important part of Chinese culture. Use the internet or other references to find out about the Chinese Lantern Festival and the Moon Festival. Find out when each festival takes place, what the festival celebrates, and what types of food are traditionally eaten.

Chinese Dishes

Starter: Potato and Tomato Soup

15 minutes preparation time
20 minutes cooking time
serves 4

Ingredients

200g tomatoes

300g potatoes

30ml vegetable oil

750ml water

1 vegetable stock cube

pinch salt

pinch pepper

Method

1   Wash the tomatoes and cut them into slices about 1cm thick.
2   Peel the potatoes and cut them into 2cm³ cubes.
3   Heat the oil and stir-fry the tomatoes until they begin to soften slightly.
4   Add the potatoes and stir-fry.
5   Add the water, stock cube, salt and pepper.
6   Bring to the boil and simmer gently for 15 minutes or until the potatoes are very soft.
7   Serve.

Main Course: Stir-fried Oyster Sauce Chicken

20 minutes preparation time
35 minutes cooking time
serves 4

Ingredients

4 chicken thighs	2.5ml salt
1.25ml black pepper, or to taste	½ onion
2 cloves garlic	1½ red peppers
125ml chicken stock	30ml oyster sauce
15ml dark soy sauce or tamari*	
15ml Chinese rice wine, dry white wine or dry sherry**	
5ml brown sugar	10ml olive oil

Notes

*   Tamari is a type of soy sauce that is made without wheat and is therefore suitable for those with certain allergies. It is dark in colour and has a rich flavour.

**   White grape juice or apple juice can be used as an alternative to alcohol.

Method

1   Rinse the chicken thighs and pat dry. Cut in half. Rub the salt and pepper over the thighs.

2   Peel and chop the onion.

3   Peel and finely chop the garlic.

4   Cut the red pepper in half, remove the seeds, and cut into 2.5cm squares.

5   In a small bowl, combine the chicken stock, oyster sauce, soy sauce, rice wine, and brown sugar. Set aside.

6   In a non-stick frying pan, heat the olive oil over medium heat. Add the chicken thighs and brown on both sides. Remove the chicken thighs from the pan and drain on paper towels. Do not clean out the pan.

7   Add the onion and garlic to the pan, and cook until the onion is softened (about 5 minutes). Add the red pepper to the pan. Cook briefly, then add the sauce.

8   Bring the sauce to the boil, then add the chicken thighs back into the pan. Reduce the heat, cover, and simmer the chicken until the juices in the thickest part of the thigh run clear when pierced with a fork (about 15 minutes). Stir the chicken occasionally while cooking.

9   Serve hot with rice.

Hints and tips

Hygiene and food safety tip

!   When using poultry remember to wash all preparation equipment after use in order to prevent the spread of bacteria. It is also important to wash your hands after touching raw poultry.

Healthy eating tip

✓   Remove the skin from the chicken thighs – either before or after cooking – to reduce the fat content of the dish.

Dessert: Chinese Almond Cookies

Chinese almond cookies are very popular biscuits in many parts of China. They are also popular as take-away foods from food stalls and supermarkets.

25 minutes preparation time
20 minutes cooking time
makes 24 cookies

Ingredients

115g butter	225g sugar
1 egg	1.25ml almond extract
140g flour	2.5ml baking powder
$\frac{1}{2}$ egg yolk	7.5ml milk
25g blanched whole almonds	15ml sesame seeds

Method

1 Set the oven to 160°C (gas mark 2–3).
2 Beat the butter and sugar in a large bowl until smooth.
3 Add the egg, almond extract and beat until well blended.
4 Beat in the flour and baking powder until well blended.
5 Cover and chill for 1 hour.
6 Shape the dough into 24 small balls and place on a baking tray 2.5 cm apart. Flatten each ball slightly.
7 Beat together the egg yolk and milk in a small bowl and brush the mixture over the prepared cookies.
8 Place a piece of almond in the middle of each cookie and sprinkle with sesame seeds.
9 Bake in the oven until lightly browned (about 15–20 minutes).
10 Remove the biscuits from the oven and cool for 5 minutes before placing onto a cooling tray.

Want to know more?

For more information about Chinese ingredients or recipes, type 'Chinese ingredients' or 'Chinese recipes' into an internet search engine, or visit the Chinese Food website.

Links to this site and other websites relating to Intermediate 2 Hospitality can be found at: www.leckieandleckie.co.uk by clicking on the Learning Lab button and navigating to the Intermediate 2 Hospitality Course Notes page.

France

Background

France is part of western Europe, only a short distance from the UK (the closest points being only 21 miles apart). It shares borders with Belgium, Luxemburg, Germany, Switzerland, Italy, Monaco, Andorra and Spain. It has the English Channel to the northwest, the Atlantic Ocean along the west coast and the Mediterranean Sea to the south. The population is similar to that of the UK, about 60 million.

French Cuisine

French cooking is considered to be the standard against which all other cuisines are measured. It is also known as **haute cuisine**. Haute cuisine was introduced into France in the 1500s by Catherine de Medici (the wife of the French King Henri II), who brought Italian chefs to France and helped to shape what would become the French classic cuisine. Haute cuisine was later adapted by Auguste Escoffier (1846–1935), who is considered the father of French cooking. In recent times **nouvelle cuisine** has been adopted to provide a light alternative to classic French cookery.

As in most countries, different regions have different food influences, determined by factors such as climate, geographical location, closeness to the sea and so on. France is no different, and each region has its own specialities:

- **Alsacienne** (Alsace region): typically involving sauerkraut and pork
- **Basquaise** (Basse-Navarre region): typically with ham and tomatoes
- **Bourguignonne** (Burgundy region): typically with red wine, bacon and onions
- **Normande** (Normandy region): typically creamy seafood sauce
- **Provençal** (Provence region): typically with olive oil, garlic and tomatoes.

Normandy is known for its rich dairy products, and its butter and cheeses are among the best in the world. The Champagne district – famous for its sparkling wines – is in the northernmost region, bordering Belgium and

Haute cuisine: *food that is prepared in an elegant or elaborate manner; the very finest food. The French word* haute *translates as 'high' or 'superior', while* cuisine *translates as 'cooking' in general.*

Nouvelle cuisine: *a modern style of French cooking that emphasises lightness of sauces and seasonings, shortened cooking times, and new and sometimes exciting combinations of foods. It translates as 'new cooking'.*

the English Channel. Legally, sparkling wine cannot be called 'champagne' unless it is produced in the Champagne region.

Fish and **seafood** are plentiful in the northern region, and the famous **Belon oysters** are shipped throughout France. Apples are grown in this region and apple brandy and apple cider are widely exported overseas.

German cuisine has influenced French cuisine in the east and northeast parts of the country, where beer, sausage, **sauerkraut** and goose are very popular. Goose fat is used for cooking. Famous dishes from these areas include **quiche Lorraine** and **pâté de fois gras**.

The area surrounding Paris is the home of classic French cuisine. This area is known for producing high quality wines, cheese, beef and veal.

The south of France borders the Mediterranean Sea, and the cuisine in this region is similar to that of Spain and Italy. Olive oil, tomatoes, garlic, herbs and fresh vegetables are all widely used. Famous dishes from this region are **black truffles, ratatouille, salade Niçoise**, and **bouillabaisse**.

The French enjoy their food and take lots of time and effort over it. Eating meals together as a family is important to the French. Wine is also an important part of French cuisine. French cuisine is also known for its special desserts such as crème brûlée and chocolate mousse.

Traditionally, the French eat three meals a day and rarely eat snacks. They usually eat a light (continental) breakfast consisting of a baguette (French bread) or croissant with butter or jam. Strong coffee or hot chocolate is popular for breakfast. For many people, lunch is the main meal of the day. Wine is drunk with both lunch and dinner, and coffee is served after both meals.

Popular French Dishes

Quiche Lorraine

A quiche is a pie made mainly of eggs and cream in a pastry crust. Other ingredients such as chopped meat or vegetables are added to the eggs before the quiche is baked. In quiche Lorraine, cream and cooked bacon are added.

Pâté de fois gras

Foie gras is the liver of a duck or a goose that has been specially fattened. Foie gras is one of the most expensive and popular French delicacies. It has a delicate but rich buttery flavour. It can be sold whole, or prepared into mousse, or pâté. It is often served as an accompaniment to another ingredients such as toast or steak. Because of the way in which the geese are reared, there is much debate about the ethics of producing foie gras.

Ratatouille

Ratatouille is a southern French dish of vegetables cooked together. A ratatouille usually includes diced onion, sautéed in oil, aubergine, garlic, green peppers, tomatoes, courgette and strongly flavoured herbs such as oregano, thyme, rosemary and basil.

Salade Niçoise

This salad is typically made with tomatoes and anchovies and is garnished with black olives and capers. The actual recipe for salade Niçoise can vary considerably from restaurant to restaurant.

Bouillabaisse

Bouillabaisse is a fish stew originating from the port city of Marseille. The base of bouillabaisse is usually a fish stock made from different kinds of cooked fish and shellfish (such as monkfish, mullet, mussels, conger eel) which are cooked with a variety of herbs and spices such as garlic, basil, bay leaf, fennel and saffron, and sometimes orange peel. Vegetables such as leeks, tomatoes, onions and celery are added to enhance the flavour.

Crème brûlée

> **Ramekin:** *a small oven-proof dish that is used to hold desserts such as a crème brûlée during cooking.*

'Crème brûlée' translates literally as 'burnt cream'. It is a dessert made from a rich custard topped with a layer of hard caramel. The caramel is made by burning a top layer of sugar under a grill or other intense heat source. It is usually served cold in individual **ramekins**. The custard base is normally flavoured only with vanilla, but other ingredients such as fruit or alcohol can be added for different flavours.

Do You Know?

- When he was American Minister to France, Thomas Jefferson (a former President of the USA) illegally smuggled rice from Italy into the USA.

- The croissant is often thought as a typical French product. In fact it is Austrian. Marie Antoinette (wife of the French King Louis XVI) brought the croissant from Vienna to Paris in 1770.

- French fries are not French either – they originated in Belgium!

- Until recently, Jacques Chirac was the French President. His favourite dish was tête de veau – calf's head.

- The French eat horse meat. Apparently this dates back to 1807 when the surgeon in charge of Napoleon's army instructed starving troops to eat the flesh of horses that had died in battle

Key Ingredients

Belon oysters

The Belon oyster is a special type of oyster from Brittany. It has a metallic flavour that is considered excellent for eating raw.

Apple brandy

Apple brandy is a dry fruit brandy made from fermented cider. It is known as calvados in France.

Sauerkraut

Sauerkraut (left) is white cabbage cut finely, salted and fermented in its own liquid.

Black truffles

Truffles (right) are very rare fungi and have a smell similar to deep-fried sunflower seeds or walnuts. Like foie gras, truffles are very expensive and are considered a delicacy in France.

Other important ingredients

Anchovy paste: made from anchovy fillets, this paste is used to add flavour to many French dishes.

Apple: a key fruit used in French cookery. Many different varieties are available, the selection depending on how it will be prepared and/or cooked.

Cheese: many different types produced; used as ingredients as well as accompaniments.

Crème fraiche: a thick, fat rich cream with a slightly sour flavour. Used as a replacment for cream in many recipes.

Garlic: used to flavour many French dishes.

Herbes de Provence: mixture of herbs such as thyme, rosemary, bay leaf and basil. Commonly used in soups, stews and roast lamb.

Lardons: small cubes of bacon that are commonly used in pasta dishes, casseroles and salads.

Mushrooms: used in many starter or savoury recipes.

Wine: many different types are produced – red, white, rosé, champagne. Some are used for cooking and other as accompaniments to French dishes.

Note: French cuisine places great emphasis on choosing fresh, high quality ingredients.

For you to do

2 Visit the Video Jug website and watch the video of how to make a salade Niçoise. What ingredients are used in this version of salade Niçoise?

Links to this site and other websites relating to Intermediate 2 Hospitality can be found at: www.leckieandleckie.co.uk by clicking on the Learning Lab button and navigating to the Intermediate 2 Hospitality Course Notes page.

3 Find out about each of the following, using either the internet or other references:
a   snuffling for truffles
b   making foie gras.

French Dishes

Starter: French Onion Soup

20 minutes preparation time
35 minutes cooking time
serves 4

Ingredients

30ml olive oil   500g onions
1 clove garlic   7.5ml brown sugar
1 litre beef stock   pinch of salt
pinch of pepper   4 slices of baguette
25g gruyère cheese*   25g parsley

Note

*Cheddar cheese can be used as an alternative.

Method

1   Finely slice the onions.
2   Grate the cheese, finely chop the parsley and crush the garlic.
3   In an oven-proof saucepan or casserole, heat the oil and add the onions. Cook over a low heat for 15 minutes until golden.
4   Add the crushed garlic and sugar.
5   Heat the beef stock and add to the onions. Mix well.
6   Bring to the boil, then turn the heat right down and simmer for 20–30 minutes.
7   Season to taste.
8   Lightly grill (or toast) the slices of baguette, and top with cheese.
9   Float the cheese-topped baguette on the soup, and place under the grill for 5 minutes, so that the cheese melts.
10   Sprinkle parsley on top and serve.

Main Course: Cauliflower au Gratin

10 minutes preparation time
40 minutes cooking time
serves 4

Ingredients

1 cauliflower   4–6 potatoes
3 onions   25ml oil
30ml corn flour   500ml milk
100g cheddar cheese   pinch of salt
pinch of pepper   pinch of nutmeg

Method

1 Preheat the oven to 220°C (gas mark 7).
2 Cut the cauliflower into small branches and wash.
3 Cook the cauliflower in boiling salted water for 10 minutes.
4 Drain the cauliflower.
5 Peel the potatoes and cook in boiling water for 15 minutes.
6 Drain and cut the potatoes into thin slices.
7 Chop the onion very finely.
8 **Sauté** the onions in a pan until tender and just lightly browned.
9 Blend the corn flour with a little of the milk in a pan.
10 Pour the remaining milk into the pan and stir over a low heat until the mixture thickens.
11 Season with salt, pepper and nutmeg.
12 Place the cauliflower and potatoes into an oven-proof dish.
13 Pour the sauce over the vegetables.
14 Grate the cheese and sprinkle it over the sauce.
15 Bake in the oven for 10 minutes.
16 Serve.

Dessert: Chocolate Mousse

15 minutes preparation time
5 minutes cooking time
serves 4

Ingredients

2 eggs   150g chocolate
30g butter   15ml sugar

Method

1 Break the chocolate into small pieces and place into a glass bowl.
2 Cut the butter into small pieces and add to the chocolate.
3 Place the bowl over a pan of boiling water and melt the chocolate and butter. Ensure that no boiling water gets into the bowl.
4 Remove from the heat.
5 Separate the eggs.
6 Add a pinch of salt to the egg whites and beat until stiff.
7 Add the yolks to the chocolate mixture, one at a time, beating well after each addition.
8 Add the sugar and beat in well.
9 Pour the chocolate mixture into a large bowl.
10 Fold in the whisked egg whites, one spoon at a time until well mixed.
11 Pour into a large serving dish or individual dishes.
12 Chill until set, then decorate as desired.

Hints and tips

Hygiene and food safety tip

! This recipe for Chocolate mousse is an example of a classical French dessert. It does, however, contain raw eggs. Raw eggs can be a source of dangerous bacteria that can cause food poisoning, especially in certain groups, such as pregnant women, the elderly, babies, toddlers and people who are ill or recovering from illness. For this reason it is common in the industry to use pasteurised egg whites (sometimes dried, sometimes frozen) in recipes such as this.

! Other foods which commonly use raw eggs include:

- freshly prepared desserts such as soufflés and mousses
- home-made ice-cream
- meringues
- home-made mayonnaise.

Want to know more?

For more information about French ingredients and French recipes, type 'French ingredients' or 'French recipes' into an internet search engine, or visit the BBC Food website.

Links to this site and other websites relating to Intermediate 2 Hospitality can be found at: www.leckieandleckie.co.uk by clicking on the Learning Lab button and navigating to the Intermediate 2 Hospitality Course Notes page.

Mexico

Background

UNITED STATES OF AMERICA

MEXICO

Gulf of Mexico

CUBA

Yucatan

Mexico City

North Pacific Ocean

Puebla　Veracruz

Acapulco　Oaxaca

BELIZE

GUATEMALA

Mexico is in North America, surrounded on the north by the United States; on the south and west by the Pacific Ocean; on the southeast by Guatemala, Belize and the Caribbean Sea, and on the east by the Gulf of Mexico. Mexico consists of 31 states and a federal district, Mexico City, one of the most populated cities in the world, with more than 19 million inhabitants.

Mexican Cuisine

Mexican food varies by region due to a number of factors including climate, geography, the ethnic differences of inhabitants and the influences of nearby countries. Mexico was under the rule of Spain for several hundred years, and this had a major influence in its cuisine.

Before the arrival of Spanish **conquerors** in the 15th century, the diet of the **Aztecs** consisted of corn-based dishes with chillies and herbs, usually with the addition of beans and squash.

> **Aztecs:** *the ancient tribe who lived in what is now known as Mexico.*
>
> **Conqueror:** *someone who has fought against and taken over control of a country or its people*

The Spanish conquerors brought new ingredients to the Aztec diet, including rice, beef, pork, chicken, wine, garlic and onions. These were then incorporated with traditional Aztec ingredients such as chocolate, **maize**, tomato, vanilla, **avocado**, **papaya**, pineapple, chilli, beans, **squash**, **sweet potato**, peanut and turkey. It is thought that the popular Mexican dish **totopo** might originate back to this time.

The Pacific coast is famous for its seafood and for **achiote** sauce, which is served with fish, chicken and pork. Mexico has many exotic fruits such as **guanabana** and **cherimoya**, and these often accompany seafood dishes

In central Mexico, there is a mixture of Spanish and Aztec cuisines: nuts, different spices, cocoa and seeds are commonly used. In the south, peppers are mostly used dry, especially in stews and toppings.

There are four main regions in Mexico, all of which provide different types of dishes, with a wide range of smells, textures and flavours: Puebla, Oaxaca, Yucatan and Veracruz.

Puebla is not far from Mexico City and its cuisine is famous for its **mole** sauce that is often used in chicken dishes, **camotes** dessert, and many pastries.

Oaxaca is famous for the Oaxaqueno mole that contains bananas, giving it a sweeter flavour. Oaxaqueno mole is traditionally served with chicken.

Yucatan has many fruit-based sauces, spread over chicken (pollo pibil), or pork (cochinita pibil).

Veracruz is located on the Pacific coast, so fish is an important part of the diet. A popular dish is fish a la Vareacruzana, which is fish topped with a local specialty – a rich, spicy tomato sauce made with herbs and spices. Although served mainly with fish this sauce can also be served with chicken.

Popular Mexican Dishes

There are many Mexican dishes that are now popular in the UK. There is a growing interest in Mexican cuisine, particularly as more and more people have the opportunity to travel to Mexico on holiday and try Mexican cuisine.

Burrito

A burrito is a white flour tortilla, which is filled with different types of meat, beans, cheese, or even a combination of these. The tortilla is then rolled tightly and often served smothered with chilli sauce and melted cheese.

Mole

Mole or mole sauce is a dark brown Mexican sauce or gravy made from dry chillies, nuts, spices, vegetables, chocolate and seasonings. Mole takes a long time to prepare, and is often served as chicken mole, or in beef or pork for special occasions and holidays. There are regional variations of mole.

Quesadilla

'Quesadilla' means 'little cheesy thing', and this dish consists of a corn tortilla filled with various ingredients including cheese. The ingredients are generally cooked after the tortilla has been filled.

Taco

A taco is a tortilla folded in half and fried until crisp. The fried tortilla is then stuffed with a mixture of meat, chicken, refried beans (beans which are mashed, then fried, often in melted animal fat), lettuce, onion, cheese, and taco sauce.

Tortilla

A tortilla (left) is a thin, flat bread made from wheat flour or corn meal. Many Mexicans prefer tortilla to our European concept of bread.

Totopo

A totopo (right) is a tortilla that is made with salt in the dough and is then baked dry, so that it has a hard texture.

Key Ingredients

Achiote
Achiote is a red paste made from the annatto seeds of the annatto tree.

Avocado
Avocado is a pear-shaped tropical fruit with a thickened skin and a green buttery flesh. It is also known as an alligator pear. It is used in many Mexican dishes, such as guacamole.

Camotes
This is a dessert made of sweet potato.

Cherimoya
Cherimoya is an exotic fruit which has a green knobbly outer skin and creamy flesh. The flesh is soft, juicy, sweet and very fragrant, and is slightly thick in texture. The flavour of the cherimoya is often described as a cross between banana, passionfruit, papaya and pineapple.

Guanabana

Guanabana is a large, dark green tropical fruit with fleshy spines on the outside and white flesh inside. It is also known as soursop.

Maize
Maize is a cereal that dates back to the time of the Aztecs. In the UK it is known as sweetcorn (and in the US simply as corn).

Papaya

Papaya is a large, pear-shaped fruit whose skin turns golden yellow when ripe. Inside, the orange-coloured flesh which surrounds small black seeds is sweet but sharp. In some countries it is called paw paw (or papaw).

Squash
Squash is a vegetable, and there are different varieties. Summer squashes tend to have thin green skins, soft seeds and pale, watery flesh, for example, the courgette. Winter squashes, however, tend to have tough, thicker skins, and are often orange or bright yellow, for example, the pumpkin.

Sweet potato
Sweet potato is a variety of potato with a thick, dark orange skin and an orange flesh that remains moist when cooked.

Other important ingredients

Annato seeds: small orange seeds with a mild flavour which are ground and used for flavour and colour.

Beans: main source of protein in Mexican cookery. Many different types are available and used in different recipes.

Chillies: many different varieties are available; these can be used raw, for example in salads, or used to provide 'heat' to many savoury dishes.

Chorizo: a type of pork sausage which is flavoured with paprika. Has a rich colour and flavour.

Masa harina: corn-based flour.

Napalitos: prickly pear cactus which is commonly cut into chunks and used in salads or as a vegetable.

Pepitas: dried pumpkin seeds which are usually ground and used to thicken sauces.

Salsa: a combination of chopped tomatoes, chillies and other spices, served as an accompaniment to savoury dishes.

Tomatoes (fresh): often used in a salsa.

Vegetable oil: commonly used in Mexican cookery; butter is seldom used. Lard is sometimes used.

Do You Know?

- Mexicans celebrate their dead ones in November in a celebration called Los Dias de los Muertos. The celebration relates to life and death and the spirits that return from the graves.
- In some parts of Mexico iguana (a type of large lizard), rattlesnakes, deer, spider monkey and even some kinds of insects are used as cooking ingredients.
- 'Tex-Mex' is a term for a type of American food which is eaten manly in Texas (USA) to describe a regional cuisine which blends American (Texan) and Mexican ingredients.
- Tequila is a type of alcohol made from a special cactus. It has its origins in Tequila, Mexico.
- According to Mexican legend, chocolate was given to the Mexicans by one of its ancient gods.
- Chewing gum was invented in Mexico in 1869!

For you to do

4 Visit the website of the School Nutrition Association. Read the article about Mexican cuisine and answer these questions.

   a What nutrients do chillies and mangoes supply?
   b What does the word 'taco' mean?
   c What is a nopal?
   d What did the English, German and French bring to Mexico?

Links to this site and other websites relating to Intermediate 2 Hospitality can be found at: www.leckieandleckie.co.uk by clicking on the Learning Lab button and navigating to the Intermediate 2 Hospitality Course Notes page.

Mexican Dishes

Starter: Mexican Stuffed Peppers

30 minutes preparation time
35 minutes cooking time
serves 4

Ingredients

4 large red or green peppers	15ml olive oil
1 onion, chopped finely	2 celery stalks, diced
5ml cumin	5ml chilli powder
5ml basil	2.5ml oregano
125g red kidney beans, cooked and drained	250g cooked brown rice
	150g tomato paste/purée

180ml tomatoes, canned, with their juice
1 pinch cayenne pepper, to taste

Method

1 Set the oven to 180°C (gas mark 4).
2 Prepare ingredients as indicated above.
3 Wash peppers and cut in half lengthways. Remove the seeds.
4 Steam the peppers, cut side down on a rack, above boiling water, until tender.
5 Heat the oil in a large pan, add the onions, celery, cumin, chilli powder, basil and oregano.
6 Sauté until the onions are tender.
7 Add the cooked rice and kidney beans. Mix well.
8 Add the cayenne pepper.
9 Lightly oil a shallow, ovenproof dish.
10 Fill each pepper with the filling and place into the baking dish.
11 Mix the tomatoes and tomato paste together and pour over the stuffed peppers.
12 Cover the peppers with foil and bake for 30 minutes.
13 Serve with a green salad.

Hints and tips

Hygiene and food safety tip

! Certain types of beans, such as kidney beans, contain toxins that can cause illness. If you plan to use dried kidney beans they need to be cooked correctly.

1 Soak the beans in water for at least 12 hours.
2 Drain the beans and rinse in cold water.
3 Boil vigorously in fresh water for at least 10 minutes.
4 Simmer for at least a further 40 minutes to make them tender.

Tinned kidney or soya beans have already been treated in this way and so are ready to use straightaway.

Main Course: La Coca (Mexican tomato and red pepper tart)

30 minutes preparation time
40 minutes cooking time
serves 4

Ingredients

2 green peppers

2 red peppers

1 onion, chopped

330g tin tomatoes

15ml olive oil

1 packet of puff pastry

Method

1   Preheat oven to 220°C (gas mark 7).

2   Brown the onion in the olive oil at a medium heat.

3   Wash and chop the peppers and add to the pan.

4   Strain the tomatoes, chop roughly and add to the pan.

5   Cover, then cook for 20 minutes over a medium heat.

6   Take lid off and cook for a further 20 minutes to reduce liquid.

7   Line a pie dish with pastry.

8   Fill with mixture.

9   Cook for 30 minutes.

10 Serve warm.

Hints and tips

Hygiene and food safety tip

!   Remember to wash all raw fruits and vegetables before use. Rinse them in cold water to remove chemical residues and other potential contaminants. Pat them dry with a disposable towel, which should also be disposed of safely.

Dessert: Mexican Cocoa Cake

20 minutes preparation time
40 minutes cooking time
serves 4

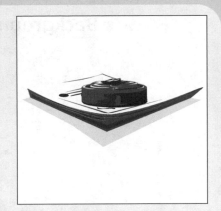

Ingredients

250g flour

80g cocoa powder

5ml baking powder

5ml baking soda

5ml cinnamon

6 egg whites

330g brown sugar

250ml yoghurt

10ml vanilla essence

1.25ml almond essence

icing sugar, sifted for decoration

Method

1   Set the oven to 180°C (gas mark 4).
2   Mix the flour, cocoa, baking powder, baking soda and cinnamon in a bowl.
3   Beat the egg whites, brown sugar, yoghurt, vanilla and almond essence until well blended.
4   Stir in the flour and beat until evenly mixed.
5   Lightly grease a 20cm square non-stick baking tin or tray.
6   Pour the prepared mixture into the tin.
7   Bake the cake for approximately 30–40 minutes or until slightly springy to touch.
8   Remove on to a serving dish when cooled slightly.
9   Dust with sifted icing sugar before serving.

Want to know more?

For more information about Mexican ingredients and Mexican recipes, type 'Mexican ingredients' or 'Mexican recipes' into an internet search engine, or visit the Mexican Grocer website.

Links to this site and other websites relating to Intermediate 2 Hospitality can be found at: www.leckieandleckie.co.uk by clicking on the Learning Lab button and navigating to the Intermediate 2 Hospitality Course Notes page.

LECKIE-&LECKIE
Learning Lab

Morocco

Background

Morocco is on the northwest coast of Africa. To the west is the Atlantic Ocean, to the north is the Mediterranean Sea, and the Sahara desert is to the south. In the centre of the country are the Atlas mountains, a mountain range which appears to split the county in half. The mountain areas are heavily populated by Islamic Berbers (the name given to the people from Morocco).

Morocco's cuisine has been influenced by other countries, such as Spain, Turkey and the Middle-East. Morocco produces all the food that it needs to feed its population. The five main products grown in Morocco are lemons, olives, figs, dates and almonds, and these are the main ingredients in many Moroccan dishes. As well as these, Morocco produces many other fruits and vegetables.

Morocco is located on the Mediterranean coast, so fish and seafood are popular in the Moroccan cuisine. Morocco is a Muslim country, so the eating of pork and the drinking of alcohol are forbidden, and these rules also influence Moroccan cuisine.

Moroccan Cuisine

Moroccans usually eat their meals at low, round tables; they generally don't use cutlery, preferring to eat with their hands (the first three fingers), specifically their right hand. Traditionally, bread is often used as a utensil, to soak up sauces and to carry the food to the mouth.

Ramadan: *a time for reflection, devotion to Allah (Muslim God), and self-control. During Ramadan, Muslims show their devotion to Allah by fasting, or abstaining from food, during daylight hours.*

The most important meal of the day for Moroccans is the midday meal, except during the holy month of **Ramadan**. The meal usually starts with a selection of salads, either cold or hot, followed by a lamb or chicken **tagine**. **Couscous** may also be served. It is traditional for sweet mint tea to be served at the end of a meal. Mint tea is made by crushing fresh mint leaves, boiling them in water and adding sugar to sweeten – usually quite a lot of sugar!

Moroccan cuisine is influenced by the cuisine of the two main royal cities of Fez and Marrakech and by the Spanish and Jewish traditions from the coastal city of Essaouira. This combination of influences can be found in four popular Moroccan dishes: **couscous**, **bisteeya**, **mechoui** and **djej emshmel**.

Spices have been imported to Morocco for many hundreds of years but much Moroccan cookery relies on home-grown produce such as mint and **olives** from Meknes, oranges and lemons from Fez, prickly pear from Casablanca and **shad** from the Sebou river. **Pomegranates**, almonds, dates, walnuts, chestnuts, honey, barley, cherries and melon are also popular in Morocco. Seafood is plentiful along the Atlantic coast while lamb and poultry are raised on higher ground.

Moroccans say that the best meals are found not in the restaurants but in the homes. Women do most of the cooking in this very traditional country.

Popular Moroccan Dishes

Bisteeya

Bisteeya is a three-layer savoury pie wrapped in the thinnest of pastry. The combination of ingredients provides an almost sweet and savoury flavour.

Couscous

Couscous is a dietary **staple** in North African countries such as Morocco and is simply coarsely ground semolina. Couscous is similar in shape and texture to rice but is smaller in size, and it is used in many dishes as rice would be.

Djej emshmel

Djej emshmel is a succulent roasted chicken cooked with olives and lemon.

Mechoui

Mechoui is tender roast lamb.

Tagine

A tagine is a type of stew cooked in a special clay cooking pot (also called a tagine). A tagine is usually made from chicken or lamb, cooked with lemons, onions, prunes and nuts. Often a tagine is garnished with slices or wedges of hard-boiled eggs. The tagine cooking pots vary in size – either individual pots for each person or, more commonly, larger pots that everyone eats from, scooping with pieces of bread.

Key Ingredients

Olive

Olives are the small oval fruit of the olive tree.
Early olives are green, mature olives are black.
Its rich oil is used for frying, marinades,
dressings and baking.

Pomegranate

Pomegranates are grown throughout Asia and the Mediterranean. They
are about the size of an orange and are composed of hundreds of little
pink/red seeds surrounded by a fruity pulp, separated by membrane. The
seeds are used in cooking but the pulp is bitter and discarded.

Prickly pear

A prickly pear is the round or pear-shaped spiny fruit of any variety of
prickly pear cacti.

Shad

Shad is a type of fish, a bit like a herring.

Do You Know?

- Almonds are an ancient food that have been written about for many centuries.
  They are produced in Morocco.
- Many Moroccans believe that the colour blue can ward off evil spirits. For this
  reason the doors of many Moroccan buildings are painted blue.
- Date palms (trees) can produce fruits for hundreds of years and there used to be a
  law in Morocco making it illegal to cut down date palms.
- The national drink of Morocco is mint tea.
- Like Scotland, football is the national sport of Morocco.

Spices

Influenced by the age-old spice trade from Arabia to North Africa, Moroccan cuisine is rich in spices which are used to enhance the flavour of food. The following spices are among the most commonly used.

Anise seed: used in breads and cookies.

Black pepper: used to season food.

Cayenne pepper: popular in the dishes of southern Morocco.

Cinnamon: used in bisteeya, couscous and many desserts.

Cumin: ground cumin is commonly used in meats, lamb and chicken.

Ginger: used in many tagines.

Paprika: used in tomato dishes and vegetable tagines.

Sesame seed: used in breads, desserts and as a garnish for savoury dishes.

Turmeric: used in harira soup, a rich, hearty soup which is the evening meal, particularly during Ramadan.

Herbs

Herbs also play an important role in Moroccan food. The following herbs are among the most commonly used.

Fragrant waters: orange flower water and rose water are used in cakes, sweets, tagines and salads.

Green coriander: the leaves, not the seeds, are often used in tagines to give them a unique flavour.

Marjoram, grey verbena and **mint:** often used in teas.

Parsley: used in tagines.

Other important ingredients

Bread: heavier Arab bread and the lighter pitta bread are both useful when eating with the fingers.

Chickpeas: used in hummus, couscous dishes and tagines.

Eggs: a very popular ingredient; curdled eggs are used in bisteeya, while vegetables and chicken are often coated with eggs.

Garlic: often used in honey dishes to balance the flavour.

Honey: used in glazed dishes, desserts, poultry stuffings and tagines.

Lemons: especially pickled lemons, used in many dishes.

Olives: popular in tagines and also as a side dish served at the start of a meal.

Onions: Spanish onions are popular.

For you to do

5 Complete the crossword below. The answers to all the questions can be found in this section on Moroccan cuisine.

Across

3   Used to make a rich type of oil.

6   A holy month in Morocco.

8   Tropical fruit consisting of hundreds of seeds surrounded by juicy flesh.

10 The Ocean to the west of Morocco.

11 Often used to glaze dishes.

12 A type of Moroccan stew.

13 A type of fish.

Down

1   Spice used in many tagines.

2   A royal city in Morocco.

4   Herb used to make tea.

5   The city where the prickly pear is found.

7   Ground semolina.

9   Tender cooked lamb.

Moroccan Dishes

Starter: Moroccan Carrot Salad

20 minutes preparation time
30 minutes cooking time
serves 4

Ingredients

500g carrots

4 cloves garlic

60ml olive oil

30ml cider vinegar

5ml ground cumin

5ml paprika

30ml chopped fresh coriander

seasoning

Method

1 Wash, peel and cut carrots into batons (jardinière).

2 Peel gloves of garlic.

3 Place carrots and garlic into saucepan with just enough water to cover.

4 Add a good pinch of salt and bring to the boil. Simmer for 7 minutes or until tender.

5 Drain carrots and garlic and place carrots into a mixing bowl.

6 Crush garlic and add to carrots.

7 Stir in the oil, vinegar, cumin, paprika and half the chopped coriander.

8 Season.

9 Place into serving dish and garnish with remaining coriander.

10 Serve either hot or cold.

Main Course: Moroccan Chicken

10 minutes preparation time
25 minutes cooking time
serves 4

Ingredients

500g chicken fillets, cut into 2cm dice

45ml plain flour

salt and pepper

60ml olive oil

2 onions, sliced

10ml ground cinnamon

1.25ml ground cloves

10ml ground sumac*

60g sultanas

250ml chicken stock

50g pine nuts

large bunch fresh coriander, chopped

1 lemon, juice of

Note

*   Sumac is a spice found in the Middle-East. If you cannot obtain it, substitute finely grated lemon rind with a pinch of salt added.

Method

1   Season flour with salt and pepper and toss chicken in it.

2   Heat half the oil in a frying pan over a high heat until hot, then cook the chicken in batches until golden. Set chicken aside.

3   Heat remaining oil in pan and add onions, reduce heat to medium, and cook for 10 minutes, stirring, until golden and softened.

4   Return chicken to pan with spices, sultanas and stock.

5   Reduce heat to low and cook for 5 minutes until heated through and thickened slightly.

6   Stir in pine nuts, coriander and lemon juice.

7   Serve with lemon wedges on side and some flat bread

Hints and tips

Hygiene and food safety tip

!   Remember that when you are using raw poultry such as chicken, you should rinse the surface of the meat with cold water to remove blood and any other possible contaminants. You should then pat the poultry dry with a disposable paper towel. Remember to dispose of the paper towel safely and to wash your hands after touching the raw poultry.

Dessert: Honey Cinnamon Oranges

10 minutes preparation time
10 minutes cooking time
serves 4

Ingredients

2 oranges

30ml honey

10ml ground cinnamon

small bunch of fresh mint leaves

Method

1 Peel the oranges and slice into thin slices (about 0.3cm thick).*

2 Place orange slices on to the serving dish.

3 Mix the honey with the cinnamon in a small dish.

4 Drizzle over the orange slices.

5 Decorate with mint leaves.

Note

* Alternatively you can 'supreme' the oranges (see page 21).

Want to know more?

For more information about Moroccan ingredients and Moroccan recipes, type 'Moroccan ingredients' or 'Moroccan recipes' into an internet search engine, or visit the Maroque website.

Links to this site and other websites relating to Intermediate 2 Hospitality can be found at: www.leckieandleckie.co.uk by clicking on the Learning Lab button and navigating to the Intermediate 2 Hospitality Course Notes page.

Greece

Background

Greece is situated in the south of Europe. It had borders with Albania, Macedonia and Bulgaria to the north, and Turkey to the east. Greece has a long coastline with the Aegean Sea to the east and south of mainland Greece, and the Ionian Sea to the west. Greece has many different islands and has a total population of some 10 million people.

Greek Cuisine

Greek cuisine is influenced by its geography and climate, its history, and the cultures of its neighbours – Turkey, the Middle-East, and the Balkan states, for example, Bulgaria. There are many similarities between Greek cuisine and the cuisines of Turks and Arabs simply because Greece is so near to these other cultures.

Greece has a warm climate and clear blue waters, meaning that it can provide a wide range of fresh produce for cooking. Olive oil is widely used in Greek cookery and is produced from the country's many olive trees. Vineyards produce good wines, lemon trees provide good fresh lemons and the seas produce a wide variety of fresh and tasty fish and seafood which are popular in the harbour-side tavernas (restaurants).

The climate is suitable for growing a wide variety of crops, and oregano, mint, basil and dill are popular herbs. Cheeses such as fresh feta, romano and kasseri are used to accompany home-made wholegrain bread or salad or are grated and used to top vegetables or pasta.

Lamb is the main meat served in Greece (the Greek word for lamb is 'arni'). Lamb is often used in Greek festivals where the whole lamb is spit-roasted out of doors. For many meals, lamb is braised or stewed in casseroles with a mixture of vegetables. Pork, beef, and game are marinated, grilled, and baked. Chicken is often braised.

Meat and vegetables are often mixed in dishes together – often served with **avgolemono**. Fresh fruit, generally figs, orange, apples and melon, usually finish the late evening dinner.

Popular Greek Dishes

Avgolemono
Avgolemono is a sauce or soup made with egg yolks and lemon mixed with broth, heated until they thicken but before they boil, so the egg doesn't curdle.

Baklava
Baklava (left) is a very famous Greek pastry. It is made with very thin layers of filo pastry filled with nuts and honey syrup. These sweet filo pastries are often used as a late afternoon meal accompanied by thick Greek coffee.

Fila pitas
Fila pitas are popular savoury, wafer-thin pastries, which are layered with chicken and mushrooms, spinach and feta, or lamb and leeks.

Greek salad
Greek salad is generally made with tomatoes, cucumber, green peppers and onions, sprinkled with oregano, and then dressed with olive oil.

Moussaka
Moussaka (left) is a typical and popular Greek dish, layered with aubergine or zucchini (courgette) and a garlic-scented meat sauce, with a custard topping.

Pilaff
Pilaff is an Armenian, Greek or southern Russian rice dish with seasonings, often with meats, vegetables or poultry added. Pilaffs are often rich in spices and nuts.

Key Ingredients

Aubergine
The aubergine is a purple-skinned fruit, but is used as a vegetable. It is also known as an eggplant.

Zucchini
The zucchini is a long summer squash with smooth, dark green skin and a slightly bumpy surface. It has a creamy white-green flesh with a bland flavour, and looks similar to a cucumber. It is also known as a courgette.

Other important ingredients and dishes

Bourekakia: filo puffed pastry dishes made with various fillings.

Dolmades: grapevine leaves stuffed with rice or meat.

Fasolada: a popular thick bean soup.

Feta: white goats cheese.

Filo: (also called 'fila' and 'phyllo') the paper-thin pastry dough used for appetisers, entrées, and desserts.

Gouvetsi: the Greek word for casserole, or baked in the oven.

Kafes: coffee.

Kakavia: a popular soup made with seafood, onions, garlic and stock.

Kalamaria: squid.

Kalamata: a popular Greek olive.

Kasseri: a creamy farm cheese with a strong flavour.

Kefalotiri: a hard, salty cheese, good for grating.

Kourabiedes: butter cookies topped with powdered sugar.

Mezethes: small savoury appetisers.

Orzo: tiny melon seed-shaped pasta.

Ouzo: a colourless alcoholic drink with a strong aniseed flavour.

Pastitsio: a layered casserole of macaroni and chopped meat, topped with a custard sauce.

Retsina: white or rosé wine flavoured with pine.

Rigani: the Greek name for oregano, used in many Greek dishes.

Skordalia: garlic sauce.

Souvlakia: skewered food.

Spanakopeta: spinach filo pastries.

Tahini: paste made of crushed sesame seeds.

Tarama: fish eggs derived from the grey mullet.

Taramosalata: fish egg spread that is a popular Greek appetiser or starter.

Tiropita: filo pastry stuffed with Greek cheese.

Tsatziki: a popular cucumber and yoghurt dip.

Yoghurt: popular in Greek cooking; is usually a thick, rich yoghurt made from sheep or goats milk.

Do You Know?

- Greek classical history suggests that feta cheese was first made by the Cyclops Polyphemus in his caves. A Cyclops is a mythical beast with only one eye.
- The word 'asparagus' (the green-stalked vegetable) comes from the Greek language and means sprout or shoot.
- Famous Greek philosophers Plato, Epicurus and Plutarch were vegetarians.
- Archestratus was a famous Ancient Greek cook (who lived in the 4th century BC) who invented unusual recipes such as fried electric eel and fried shark.

For you to do

6 Complete the wordsearch which contains herbs and spices traditionally used in Greek cookery. Find these words:

anise	basil	cinammon
cloves	dill	fennel
mahlab	marjoram	mastic
nutmeg	oregano	purslane
rocket	sumac	tarragon
thyme	vanilla	

K	M	A	R	J	O	R	A	M	C	G	W	Y	B	L
H	J	R	Y	O	Q	R	V	S	X	J	F	I	G	E
C	C	L	P	M	L	O	S	U	M	A	C	M	C	A
R	Q	O	W	T	U	C	T	M	A	H	L	A	B	B
K	J	T	E	O	E	K	S	A	L	L	C	S	N	C
Y	C	N	U	E	T	E	S	O	N	H	V	T	T	Q
N	N	G	P	H	C	T	H	Y	M	E	C	I	A	C
L	Z	N	K	J	I	O	J	R	G	C	P	C	R	I
N	U	T	M	E	G	R	C	D	I	L	L	K	R	N
H	Z	V	A	S	M	E	F	E	N	N	E	L	A	N
W	V	L	N	Z	H	G	W	N	M	R	Z	A	G	A
E	B	A	I	I	V	A	N	I	L	L	A	C	O	M
P	U	R	S	L	A	N	E	B	A	S	I	L	N	O
O	J	N	Γ	I	Γ	O	Z	W	W	C	O	D	V	N
C	Y	D	D	V	C	L	O	V	E	S	Y	K	T	O

Greek Dishes

Starter: Chickpea Bourekia

30 minutes preparation time
30 minutes cooking time
serves 6

Ingredients

225g tinned chickpeas

30ml olive oil

1 onion, chopped finely

1 clove of garlic, crushed

2 tomatoes, finely chopped

seasoning

125ml white wine or vegetable stock

125g feta cheese

15ml fresh coriander, chopped

1 egg, beaten

225g filo pastry

Method

1   Prepare all ingredients as specified above.
2   Set oven to 190°C (gas mark 5).
3   Mash the chickpeas in a bowl and set aside.
4   Heat the olive oil in a pan and gently cook the onions and garlic until tender.
5   Add the tomatoes, seasoning and stir well.
6   Add the wine or stock and simmer for 5 minutes. Remove from the heat.
7   Stir in the cheese, chickpeas, coriander and egg.
8   Adjust seasoning if required.
9   Cut the filo pastry into 10cm x 20cm rectangles.
10 Brush each rectangle with olive oil and place a spoonful of the filling on to one end of the sheet.
11 Fold over the sides of the pastry and roll into a sausage shape.
12 Bake for 15 minutes or until golden in colour.

Hints and tips

Filo pastry is very difficult to make. Buy it ready made, either fresh or frozen.

Main Course: Greek Fish

10 minutes preparation time
25 minutes cooking time
serves 4

Ingredients

250ml lemon juice

10ml olive oil

1.25 ml dried oregano

500g cod fillets

bunch of spinach leaves

50g olives

1 lemon, cut into wedges

Method

1   Mix the lemon juice, olive oil and oregano in a small bowl.

2   Wash and pat dry the cod fillets and place into a deep-sided frying pan.

3   Pour the oil mixture over the cod.

4   Bring to the boil, reduce the heat and simmer for 5 minutes or until the fish begins to flake.

5   Line the serving plate with the spinach leaves.

6   Place the fish on the spinach and pour the cooking liquid over the fish.

7   Garnish with the olives and lemon wedges.

Hints and tips

Hygiene and food safety tip

!   Remember to wash the lemon before using as a garnish. This will help to remove any chemical residues and also any wax covering that may be found on the lemon skin.

Dessert: Greek Almond Honey Cake

20 minutes preparation time
1 hour and 15 minutes cooking time
serves 8

Ingredients

225g unsalted butter

225g caster sugar

3 eggs, lightly beaten

225g ground almonds

2 oranges, grated zest and juice

115g semolina flour

5ml baking powder

pinch of salt

75ml Greek honey*

1 large orange, juice only

Note

* Any type of honey can be used in place of Greek honey.

Method

1   Preheat the oven to 160°C (gas mark 3). Butter and flour a 25cm loose-bottomed cake tin.

2   Lightly beat the eggs, zest and juice the two oranges.

3   Using an electric whisk, beat together the butter and sugar in a large mixing bowl until pale and light.

4   Gradually beat in the eggs and stir in the ground almonds.

5   Fold in the orange juice and zest, semolina, baking powder and salt.

6   Spoon into the prepared cake tin and bake for about 1 hour and 15 minutes, or until just set and golden brown. (When cooked, a skewer inserted into the cake should come out clean.)

7   Warm the honey and the juice of the other orange in a small pan.

8   Arrange a slice of cake on a serving plate. Drizzle over the warm honey syrup.

9   Serve with Greek yoghurt and thyme leaves.

Want to know more?

For more information about Greek ingredients and Greek recipes, type 'Greek ingredients' or 'Greek recipes' into an internet search engine, or visit the Greek Food website.

Links to this site and other websites relating to Intermediate 2 Hospitality can be found at: www.leckieandleckie.co.uk by clicking on the Learning Lab button and navigating to the Intermediate 2 Hospitality Course Notes page.

Herbs

There are many different herbs used in the different world cuisines. The following list describes some of the most popular.

Basil

Basil (*Ocimum basilicum*) is a bright green, leafy plant, and is part of the mint family. It has a strong, sweet flavour, and can smell grassy and hay-like, with a hint of mint. It is best used fresh.

Bay leaf

Bay leaves come from the sweet bay or laurel tree (*Laurus nobilis*). The leaves are dull green in colour, have a glossy surface, and grow up to 8cm long. The leaves are characterised by a green, woody and sharp flavour, and have a pleasant, slightly minty taste. They are best used dried.

Coriander

Coriander (*Coriandrum sativum*), also known as cilantro, is the leaf of the young coriander plant, which is a member of the parsley family. It is light to medium-green in colour. The flavour and aroma of the coriander leaf is generally described as being waxy, citrus and soapy in nature. The flavour of the leaf is quite different from the seed.

Dill

Dill (*Anethum graveolens*) is a tall, feathery member part of the parsley family. The seeds (light brown) and the leaves or weed (medium to dark green) come from the same dill plant. The leaves are fresher in flavour than the seeds, and are characterised by sweet, grassy, tea-like/rye notes. The leaves are best used fresh, while the seeds are used whole.

Marjoram

Marjoram (*Majorana hortensis*) is the light grey-green leaf of a low growing member of the mint family. It has a delicate, sweet, minty flavour with a slightly bitter undertone. It is often mistaken for oregano. It can be used fresh or dried.

Mint

There are more that 30 different varieties of mint, but two of the most important are *Mentha spicata L.* (spearmint) and *Mentha piperita L.* (peppermint). The leaves range in colour from light green to dark green. Mint is strong and sweet with a tangy flavour and a cool aftertaste. The leaves are best used fresh.

Oregano

Mediterranean oregano is the leaf of *Origanum vulgare L.*, a herb in the mint family. Mexican oregano is the dried leaf of one of several plants of the Lippia genus. The leaves range in colour from light to dark green, and flavour resembles marjoram but is not as sweet. Oregano has a strongly aromatic smell and a slightly bitter, spicy flavour. It can be used fresh or dried.

Parsley

There are many different parsley varieties, but the two most common are *Petroselinum crispum* (curly leaf) left, and *Petroselinum neapolitanum* (flat leaf) right. The colour of the leaf is bright to dark green, and it has a mildly peppery flavour. It is best used fresh, as dried is a very poor substitute.

Rosemary

The leaves of the rosemary plant (*Rosmarinus officinalis*) are green-grey in colour, and have an aromatic, woody, pine-like flavour, with a hint of lemon. Rosemary can be used fresh or dried.

Sage

Sage (*Salvia officinalis*) is a shrub, but is actually part of the mint family. It has long, grey-green leaves which have a velvety, cotton-like texture when rubbed. It is highly aromatic and has a medicinal, pine-like, woody, slightly bitter flavour. It can be used fresh or dried.

Tarragon

Tarragon (*Artemisia dracunculus*) is a small, shrubby herb. The leaves are green, and have an aromatic, liquorice-like flavour and aroma, with a hint of mint. Two species are grown – Russian and French. Leaves of the French variety are shinier and stronger smelling. Most commercial tarragon comes from dried leaves of the French variety. Tarragon can be used fresh or frozen.

Thyme

Thyme is the leaf of a shrub in the mint family called *Thymus vulgaris*. It has small grey-green leaves, with a minty, lemony flavour. For use as a condiment, thyme leaves are dried, then chopped or ground. Thyme can be used fresh or dried.

Hints and tips

If you want a herb to contribute a gentle background flavour, add a sprig at the beginning of cooking. For a stronger herb flavour, chop the herb and add it near the end of cooking.

For you to do

1 Follow these instructions and make some herb tea.
   - Place a few leaves of fresh mint, thyme, sage or lavender flower into a cup.
   - Pour in boiling water and cover with a saucer.
   - Leave for about 3–4 minutes.
   - Strain and drink.

   Did you like your herb tea? Explain your answer.

Want to know more?

This is not an exhaustive list of herbs. Type 'herbs' into an internet search engine if you want to find out more about the extensive range of herbs available around the world.

Spices

There are many different spices used in the different world cuisines. The following list describes some of the most popular.

Anise seed

Anise is the dried, ripe fruit of the *Pimpinella anisum* plant. The seeds are green-brown in colour, are crescent-shaped and have a liquorice-like flavour and aroma. Anise is used whole or crushed in cookies, cakes, breads, cheese, pickles, stews, fish and shellfish. Middle-East, Portuguese, German, Italian and French cuisines use anise in seasoning blends such as curry, hoisin, sausage and pepperoni.

Black pepper

Black pepper comes from the small, dried berries of the *Piper nigrum* vine. The berries are picked while green and are allowed to ferment, before being sun-dried until they shrivel and turn a brownish-black colour. They have a sharp, hot, pine-like taste. Peppercorns can be used whole, or can be crushed or ground to add heat and flavour to cooking. Freshly ground peppercorns have much more flavour than ready-ground pepper,

Cayenne

Cayenne (*Capsicum annuum*) is a very hot and powerful spice, and is made by grinding the pod and seeds of dried chillies. Its colour ranges from orange to deep red, and it has a hot and sharp flavour and aroma. It is often used in curries.

Cinnamon

Cinnamon (*Cinnamomum verum*) is a sweet, warm spice which comes from the bark of a tree commonly found in Sri Lanka. The bark is removed, dried and rolled up to make a hollow tube. In cookery, it is mainly used to flavour desserts, chocolate, sweets and some alcoholic drinks. In the Middle-East, it is often used in savoury dishes such as chicken and lamb. Cinnamon is available ground (powdered) as well as in sticks.

Cumin

Cumin seeds come from a plant called *Cuminum cyminum* and are used for their strong, unique flavour. Cumin is popular in north African, Middle-Eastern, western Chinese, Mexican and Indian cuisines (it is a key ingredient in Indian curries). The seeds are light grey-brown in colour, while ground (powdered) cumin is yellow-brown.

Ginger

Ginger comes from the thick underground stem (rhizome) of the *Zingiber officinale* plant. Ginger is commonly used to add warmth to both sweet and savoury dishes and is used in cuisines throughout Asia and Europe. It is light brown in colour, and has a slightly citrus/soapy flavour. Ginger can be used fresh (often called root ginger or ginger root) or dried and ground to a powder.

Paprika

Paprika is the bright red powder made by grinding dried bell peppers (*Capsicum annuum*). Although from the same family, it is much milder than cayenne pepper, adding a slight sweetness to savoury dishes. It is often used in beef, lamb, chicken and fish dishes.

Sesame seed

Sesame is the dried, oval-shaped seed of the plant *Sesamum indicum*. The seeds are light in colour, and have a mildly nutty flavour. Sesame seeds can be made into a paste called tahini (used in hummus) and a Middle-Eastern sweet called halvah. East Asian cuisines use sesame oil and sesame seeds to flavour savoury dishes (the Koreans use sesame to marinate meat and vegetables, while the Chinese use it in dim sum dishes and sesame seed balls). The seeds can be used plain or roasted.

Turmeric

This is a bright yellow spice that comes from the thick underground stem (rhizome) of a plant from the ginger family. Turmeric is often an ingredient in curry powder and it's used on its own in many Asian dishes, including fish curries, dhals, pilafs as well as in many north African meat and vegetable dishes. Turmeric can be bough fresh but it is often bought dried and ground, in powder form.

For you to do

2 As well as being important ingredients that provide flavour and colour to dishes, spices are also known for their health benefits. Use the internet or other reference to find out the possible health benefits of these common spices:

  a ginger

  b turmeric

  c cinnamon

If you need help, try looking up the Six Wise website.

If you want more information on spices, visit the McCormick website.

Links to these sites and other websites relating to Intermediate 2 Hospitality can be found at: www.leckieandleckie.co.uk by clicking on the Learning Lab button and navigating to the Intermediate 2 Hospitality Course Notes page.

LECKIE&LECKIE
Learning Lab

Fruit

There are many different types of fruit available across the world. The following list describes some of the most popular, as well as some of the more unusual.

Fig

Although thought of as a fruit, the fig is actually the flower of the fig tree. The fresh fig 'fruit' is soft, juicy and very sweet, and is full of small seeds. Figs can be eaten dried as well as fresh. Figs range in colour (from green to very deep purple) and texture depending upon the variety. The fig originates from south-west Asia and the Eastern Mediterranean.

Granadilla

Granadilla is orange or yellow coloured and has a round shape with a tip sticking out from the end. The outer skin is hard and shiny, and has a soft inner skin to protect the seeds. The hard, black seeds are surrounded by a clear pulp, which is the edible part of the fruit. Granadilla has a strong acidic taste with a sweet aroma. Granadilla originates in the Andes region of South America.

Guava

The guava is a pear- or round-shaped fruit with a yellow-green outer skin and pale yellow flesh which contains edible seeds. The guava has a very attractive smell and a sweet-acid taste. The guava originates from Brazil and South Africa.

Kiwi fruit

Sometimes known as the Chinese gooseberry, kiwi fruit is named after the famous New Zealand bird because of its furry brown skin. The kiwi fruit has a fresh tangy flavour with a bright green flesh. The flesh has many hundreds of small edible black seeds in the centre. The young kiwi fruit is quite acidic, but mellows as it ripens.

Kumquat

The kumquat is closely related to citrus fruits, and looks like a very small orange. The rind is thin and edible with a sweet but sharp, sour flavour. Kumquats originate from China and were thought to be symbols of gold and good fortune.

Lychee

Fresh lychees (litchis) are round with red-brown skin and cloudy white flesh which has jelly-like texture. The centre of a lychee contains a hard inedible brown seed. Lychees have a slightly perfumed flavour. Lychees originate from China and were considered a symbol of love and romance by the Chinese for centuries.

Mango

The mango is a sweet-smelling tropical fruit, whose skin ranges in colour from yellow-green to dark red. The flesh is yellow/light orange with a distinct flavour similar to apricot and pineapple; the aroma can be described as sweet yet resinous or oily. The mango originates from the Far East.

Papaya

The papaya is a pear-shaped fruit with a yellow-orange skin. When it is ripe, it has a pink-orange flesh and dark inedible seeds inside. Its flavour is similar to peaches and apricots. Confusingly, papaya is known as pawpaw (or papaw) in some countries, but in other countries, pawpaw is a completely different fruit. Papaya originates from South America.

Passion fruit

The passion fruit is a tropical, egg-shaped fruit which, when ripe, has a hard, purple-brown, wrinkled outer skin (it looks like a shrivelled plum). The flesh is yellow and juicy with edible seeds. Passion fruit has a sweet-acid flavour with a very fragrant fruity smell. It originates from Brazil.

Physalis

Also known as a cape gooseberry, physalis are small orange fruits similar in size and shape to cherry tomatoes. The fruit is partly or fully covered in a papery leaf. The flavour of the physalis resembles both the tomato and the pineapple. The physalis is tropical, originating in North, Central and South America, but it is also grown in many subtropical countries.

Star fruit

Also known as the carambola, this yellow-green fruit has a star shape and a thin waxy skin. The colour changes to yellow as it ripens. Star fruit have a sharp, bittersweet flavour. The fruit can be sliced through to achieve a star shape. The star fruit originates from South-East Asia.

Tamarillo

The tamarillo is also known as the tree tomato, as it comes from the same family as the tomato and has a similar taste. Tamarillo are shaped like eggs and have a hard red or yellow skin. The yellow fruits are usually sweeter than the red. The flesh is juicy with many small edible seeds. The tamarillo originates from South America.

For you to do

3 Visit the website of the Fruit Pages, and find out about these unusual fruits:

  a durian

  b xigua

  c ugli.

Links to this site and other websites relating to Intermediate 2 Hospitality can be found at: www.leckieandleckie.co.uk by clicking on the Learning Lab button and navigating to the Intermediate 2 Hospitality Course Notes page.

LECKIE&LECKIE
Learning Lab

Vegetables

There are many different types of vegetable available across the world. The following list describes some of the most popular, as well as some of the more unusual.

Aubergine

Also known as eggplant, aubergines are commonly used in Mediterranean countries and also India. There are different varieties and colours of aubergine but the most common variety in the UK is the deep purple aubergine which has a long fat shape. Aubergines can have a bitter flavour and so are usually salted before use to remove the bitter juices.

Celeriac

This is a large root vegetable which has a very knobbly outer skin. Celeriac has a peppery flavour similar to celery with a slightly nutty taste. It is prepared in a similar way to a potato. It can be boiled, roasted, mashed or steamed, and is commonly made into soup.

Celery

Celery is actually a member of the carrot family, although it looks nothing like a carrot. Celery has either pale green or yellow firm and ribbed stalks which usually have small yellow leaves. It has a firm texture and slightly peppery flavour. Celery is used to flavour soups, stews and casseroles as well as being used raw.

Globe artichoke

The globe artichoke is a type of thistle – the globe-shaped part (stalk) of the artichoke is removed, leaving the inner heart. Globe artichoke has a clear green colour. The leaves are normally cooked in salted boiling water for about 35 minutes and served hot or cold. The leaves can be peeled, dipped into a serving sauce and the fleshy part sucked out. The globe artichoke originated from North America but is now available in Europe and South America.

Jerusalem artichoke

The Jerusalem artichoke is a tuber (root-like) vegetable that has a knobbly appearance and is light brown or brown-red on the outside. The flesh is creamy in colour. This type of artichoke is peeled thinly before being boiled, steamed, deep-fried, sautéd or roasted. It originates from North America but is now grown in Europe.

Mange tout

Mange tout is also known as snow pea, sugar pea or Chinese pea. It is a popular vegetable in the UK, China and France. It is a green vegetable that consists of a small flat green pod containing very small, undeveloped peas. Mange tout have a sweet, pea-like flavour. In French 'mange tout' means 'eat all'. Once cooked in boiling water, steamed or added to a stir fry, you eat the whole vegetable – the pod and the peas.

Okra

Okra is also known as ladies' finger or gumbo. Because they contain seeds, they are technically fruit rather than vegetables, but they are listed here with vegetables because of the way they are prepared and used in cooking. Okra are small, dark green ribbed seed-containing pods about 8cm in length; both pods and seeds are eaten. Okra can be added to soup and stews or served as a vegetable in its own right. Okra originate from the Ethiopian Highlands, but are also grown in the Middle-East, the Americas and the West Indies.

Pak choi

Pak choi is a green, leafy member of the cabbage family, with long, green, ribbed stalks and soft, oval-shaped leaves. It has a delicate flavour and can be steamed or stir-fried for best results. It is especially popular in Asian cookery.

Parsnip

Parsnips are a winter root vegetable, but are now available throughout the year. They are a member of the carrot family. Parsnips are a pale yellow-cream in colour, with a tough cream-coloured flesh. Parsnips need to be peeled before use, and they can be boiled, roasted, baked, boiled or mashed. When cooked, the flesh becomes tender, and they have a sweet flavour.

Spinach

Spinach is a popular leafy vegetable, which wilts and reduces in volume quite dramatically when cooked. Summer spinach is light green and fine whereas winter spinach is darker and coarser. It has a higher iron content than most green vegetables.

Sweet potato

Despite its name, sweet potato isn't actually a member of the potato family, but it is a root vegetable that is similar to the potato. Sweet potato tends to be longer in shape, with a pink-orange skin and a deep orange flesh. Sweet potatoes have a sweet flavour and a creamy, light texture. Sweet potatoes can be cooked in the same ways as plain potatoes.

Yam

The yam is shaped like a small but long rugby ball. It has a tough, outer brown skin with a flesh that can vary in colour from white to purple. Yams are cooked in their skins and then peeled, but can also be peeled and boiled. They can be used in the same way as potatoes. The yam is a popular food in the Caribbean and other tropical countries.

For you to do

4 Make a list of vegetables beginning with the letter P.
   Try to get at least seven.

Meat

Different animals are used throughout the world as a food source. The most common are listed below, but there are many more.

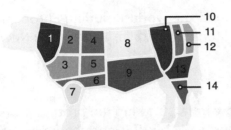

1 Neck and clod	5 Thin rib	10 Rump
2 Chuck and blade	6 Brisket	11 Silverside
3 Thick rib	7 Shin	12 Topside
4 Fore rib	8 Sirloin	13 Thick flank
	9 Flank	14 Leg

Beef

Beef is the name for the meat that comes from cattle. Beef is one of the main meats used in Europe and America and is important in the cuisine of Africa, east Asia, and South-East Asia. Some countries do not eat beef for religious or cultural reasons. Beef can be used in many different ways, from steaks and roasts to mince and sausages. The organs can also be eaten – heart, kidney and liver. The better cuts of meat, such as sirloin, are usually obtained from the young bull (male), as the younger females tend to be kept for breeding. Older animals are used for beef when they are no longer suitable for breeding. The meat from older cows and bulls is generally tougher, so it is often used for mince and meat products. Different cuts of beef come from different parts of the animal, as shown.

Lamb and mutton

The meat of a sheep one year old or younger is generally known as lamb, whereas the meat of an older sheep is known as mutton, depending on its age and characteristics. Lamb and mutton are popular in cuisines of the Mediterranean, north Africa, the Middle-East, south Asia and certain parts of China because other red meats are not eaten for religious or economic reasons. Lamb is often divided into three different kinds of meat: forequarter (which includes the neck, shoulder, front legs and the ribs up to the shoulder blade), the hindquarter (which includes the rear legs and hip), and the loin (which includes the ribs between the two).

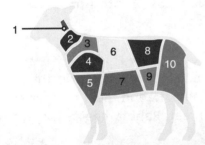

1 Neck	4 Shoulder	8 Loin
2 Middle neck	5 Shank	9 Flank
3 Best end of neck	6 Rack/Rib	10 Leg
	7 Breast	

Pork

Pork is the name for meat which comes from the pig. It is one of the most common meats consumed. Like beef, it is not eaten in some countries for religious and cultural reasons. Pork is a common meat in the diet of western countries but is also popular in other countries such as China, Vietnam and Korea. Pork may be cooked from fresh meat or it can be cured over time. Cured meat products include ham and bacon. Different cuts of pork come from different parts of the pig, as shown.

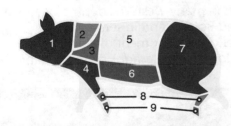

1 Head	4 Hand	7 Leg/Ham
2 Spare rib roast	5 Loin	8 Hock
3 Blade	6 Belly	9 Trotters

Deer

Venison is the name given to meat obtained from deer. It can be eaten in a number of ways – as a steak, roast, sausage, mince or in a casserole. It has a similar flavour to beef, although it is richer, but is much leaner.

Venison is eaten in many countries around the world including European countries, USA, Canada, China, Russia, Korea, Australia, Taiwan and New Zealand.

Horse

Horse meat is slightly sweet, tender, low in fat, and high in protein. Horse is eaten in many countries in Europe and Asia, but it is not generally eaten in the UK, USA or Australia. Horse meat is not generally eaten in Spain, although the country exports horses to France and Italy where they are eaten. Horse meat is also eaten in some Latin American countries such as Mexico.

Goat

The taste of goat meat is similar to that of lamb. In some parts of Asia, such as India, the word 'mutton' is used to describe both goat and lamb meat. Goat can be stewed, baked, grilled, barbecued, minced or even made into sausages. In India, goat meat is used as an ingredient in the preparation of rice for mutton biryani because it helps produce a rich taste. Goat meat is also popular in the Middle-East, South Africa, other African countries, Brazil and the West Indies.

Rabbit

Rabbit is popular as a food source in Europe, South America, North America, in parts of the Middle-East and China. Rabbit meat can generally be used in much the same way as chicken meat. Rabbit meat is leaner than beef, pork or chicken meat.

Do You Know?

Other animals used for food include:
- yak: a long-haired, humped, domestic cow-like animal found in Tibet and throughout the Himalayan areas. Yaks are kept for both their meat and milk
- guinea pig: a rodent (or pest) commonly kept as a pet in many western countries. Guinea pigs are an important meat source in parts of Peru and Bolivia, and in some areas of Ecuador and Columbia. The meat is similar to rabbit and the dark meat of chicken. Guinea pig meat may be served fried (*chactado* or *frito*), broiled (*asado*), or roasted (*al horno*), and in city restaurants may also be served in a casserole or a fricassée.

For you to do

5 Use the internet or other reference to find out the range of animals that are eaten for their meat throughout the world. (You may find it helpful to type 'list of meat animals' into a search engine.) Name another five types of animals eaten for their meat.

Fish and Shellfish

There are many hundreds of different types of fish around the world. Some types of fish come from the sea, others from rivers, some are shellfish, some are flat-shaped fish and some are round-shaped fish. The following list includes fish that are commonly used in the UK as well as some more unusual fish from other countries.

Anchovy

Anchovy is a small, round oily fish which is usually filleted and cured (preserved) by salting or brining (being soaked in salted water), before being bottled or canned. The anchovy fish is green but turns black/dark brown when cured. Anchovy is often used as an appetiser, to garnish dishes such as pizza, or, in paste form, to add a salty fishy flavour to some dishes. The anchovy is a member of the herring family and is common in the Mediterranean Sea and the English Channel.

Cod

Cod is a very popular round-shaped fish which has a dark silver/grey skin and firm white flesh with a mild flavour. It is used as a fish is its own right, but it is also used in fish products such as fishcakes and fish fingers. Cod can be bought as steaks, fillets or whole, and it can be baked, poached, grilled or fried – both shallow-fried and deep-fried in batter. Cod is commonly used in fish and chip shops in England, whereas haddock is used in Scotland. Cod is also popular in Europe and the USA.

Grouper

Grouper is a round-bodied fish found in the warm waters of the Atlantic, the Gulf of Mexico and the Caribbean. It is a member of the bass family. Groupers vary in size and colour, but are commonly red/orange. They have a firm white flesh and can be sold whole, in fillets or in steaks. Groupers can be baked, steamed, poached, grilled or fried.

Haddock

Haddock is a common white fish in the northern hemisphere. It is similar to cod, but is much smaller. The fish has silver scales with a distinctive black dark streak running down its back. Haddock has a firm white flesh that makes it ideal for deep-frying – and it is a popular fish in Scottish fish and chip shops. Haddock can be steamed, baked, grilled or poached.

Lobster

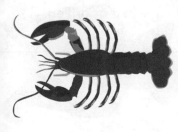

Lobster is a shellfish which is known for its sweet taste and for being expensive. The European and the American lobster are the most popular varieties. Lobster varies in colour from black to dark blue to reddish brown. When cooked, it changes to a bright red/pink colour with sweet, firm flesh. Lobsters are best bought and then cooked alive, but can be bought frozen. Lobster can be boiled (either from its live state or already dead) or grilled. The lobster tails and claws provide most of the flesh for eating.

Mackerel

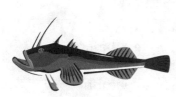

Mackerel is a small, round, oily sea fish. It has silver scales and blue/black markings on its back. The flesh is pale – sometimes pink – which when cooked becomes firm and flaky with a cream colour. Like most oily fish, mackerel has a rich flavour. Mackerel can be bought fresh or frozen and comes whole, in fillets or in steaks. It can be cooked by most cooking methods.

Monkfish

Monkfish (sometimes called an angler fish) is a very ugly fish with a large head. Monkfish is found in the Mediterranean Sea and the Atlantic Ocean. Usually only the tail of the monkfish is eaten, in the form of fillets. The fillets can be grilled, fried, poached or baked, and, when cooked, the flesh is firm and white. Monkfish tastes similar to lobster.

Prawn

Prawns are small shellfish and are a member of the lobster family. Small prawns are known as shrimp. Prawns are common in the North Atlantic as well as the Indian and Pacific Oceans. Prawns come in many different sizes, from the smaller Atlantic prawns to the large king prawns found in the Mediterranean. Prawns have a dark blue/grey colour which changes to a red/pink colour on cooking. Prawns can be bought fresh or frozen, alive or dead. They are generally grilled or fried if bought fresh, but can also be used in stews and stir-fries, or poached, steamed or baked. Prawn meat is slightly sweet and delicate in flavour.

Salmon

Salmon is a round, oily fish that is very popular in the UK – Scotland is famous for its salmon. Salmon is a freshwater fish, but it does migrate to saltwater to grow, before returning to freshwater to breed. Freshwater salmon is expensive, but farmed salmon is much cheaper. Salmon has a bright silvery skin with a deep pink flesh. Salmon has a mild to rich flavour and a tender, flaky texture. It can be bought frozen or fresh, whole or in fillets, steaks or even tinned. Salmon can be grilled, baked, fried or poached. Salmon from Canada, Japan and Norway tends to have less flavour than Scottish salmon.

Skate

Skate is a flat, kite-shaped saltwater fish. Its upper side is blue/grey in colour whereas the underside is grey/white. The 'wings' of the fish are the parts that are eaten. When cooked, they are white, have a semi-firm texture, and a slightly sweet flavour. Skate can be fried, poached or grilled.

Squid

Also known as calamari, squid is often described as a shellfish although it is actually a mollusc (it does not have a hard outer shell). There are many different types of squid found in Argentina, Mexico, Japan and the Mediterranean. The tentacles and the body pouch are the only part of the squid that are eaten. When cooked the flesh is white or creamy, and the texture should be firm but not tough. The tentacles are usually chopped and the pouch sliced into rings, or kept whole and stuffed. Squid is generally fried or stir-fried, poached or stewed.

Trout

Trout is a round, oily fish that is found in many different parts of the world. There are many different types of trout, including brown trout and rainbow trout. Rainbow trout has pinkish red stripes on the side of its silver body, whereas brown trout has a brown colour. Depending on the variety, trout flesh can vary in colour from white to orange or pink. Trout has a mild but rich flavour, and a tender but flaky texture. It can be grilled, baked, fried or poached and can be bought fresh or frozen.

For you to do

6 All types of fish have to be caught from the sea (saltwater) or a river or lake (freshwater). Some species have been over-fished and so are now scarce. To overcome this scarcity, some types of fish are now farmed. Visit the Guardian Unlimited website, read the article on fish farming, and answer these questions.

   a What types of fish are farmed?

   b What proportion of fish consumption comes from farmed fish?

   c List two advantages of fish farming.

   d List two disadvantages of fish farming.

   Then play the fish game.

   If you want to know more about sea fish, visit the Sea Fish website.

   Links to these sites and other websites relating to Intermediate 2 Hospitality can be found at: www.leckieandleckie.co.uk by clicking on the Learning Lab button and navigating to the Intermediate 2 Hospitality Course Notes page.

Dairy Products

'Dairy products' is the term used to describe food products that are made from milk. In the UK milk mainly comes from cows, but in other parts of the world, it comes from other animals as well, such as sheep, goats, horses and water buffalo. Dairy products are common in most cuisines with the exception of East Asia.

Butter

Butter is made by churning cream until the fat breaks down to create a smooth paste. There are two main types of butter:

- lactic butter: made from cream to which lactic acid bateria are added. The butter tends to be yellow in colour and can be salted or unsalted
- sweet cream butter: made in the same way as lactic butter but without the bacteria. This results in a lighter coloured butter which is normally salted.

Spreadable butter is made by adapting the churning process in a way that produces butter with a softer texture, making it easier to spread.

Margarine is different from butter. It is made from a mixture of vegetable oils, skimmed milk, salt and emulsifiers (which stops the margarine from separating). There are three main types of margarine:

- hard margarine: bought in blocks and is hard at room temperature. It is generally used for cooking and baking
- spreading margarines: used for spreading on toast, for example. These are generally spreadable even when just removed from the fridge
- margarines made from oils such as sunflower oil and olive oil are considered healthier, and can be used for spreading or baking and cooking.

Low-fat spreads are different from both margarine and butter. They are made from vegetable oils and skimmed milk but contain half the quantity of fat that is found in margarine. They can have a high water content, making them unsuitable for cooking and/or baking.

Cheese

Cheese is a popular dairy product made from milk. There are hundreds of different varieties of cheeses but there are three main categories:

- soft cheeses: these have a moisture content above 55%, so they tend to have a soft or creamy texture. Examples include:
  - goats cheese – usually very fresh cheeses of under 7 weeks' maturity
  - mould-ripened cheeses which are usually sprayed with a mould prior to maturing, for example, Brie
  - pasta filata cheese, such as Mozzarella, where the cheese is stretched in warm water to give what looks like a plastic cheese but which is in fact a creamy, full-flavoured cheese

- whey cheese, such as ricotta – made with cheese whey and only a small amount of milk. Ricotta is a white cheese with a mild, creamy flavour. It is used as an ingredient in lasagne.
- semi-hard cheeses: these have a moisture content of 44–55%, producing a semi-firm but open textured cheese. Examples include:
  - St Paulin – this is made from cows milk and is usually a wheel shape. It has a thin, washed rind which is smooth but slightly tough. St Paulin varies in colour from pale yellow to bright orange
  - Gouda – this cheese is round with a smooth, yellow, waxed rind and a sweet, fruity flavour
  - Stilton – this is a blue-mould cheese with a rich creamy flavour and a strong, sometimes bitter, aftertaste. It has narrow, blue veins and an inedible rind. The veins are caused by injecting mould into the cheese before storage
- hard cheeses: these have a moisture content of 20–43%, producing a very firm cheese. Examples include:
  - Cheddar – the colour of Cheddar ranges from white to pale yellow. Some Cheddars have a colour added, giving the cheese a yellow-orange colour. Cheddar is always made from cows milk and has a slightly crumbly texture
  - Grana padano – also known as Parmesan, this has a thick, hard rind while the cheese itself is pale yellow, hard and crumbly. The cheese should taste fresh and fruity with a hint of pineapple. It has a very strong smell.

Cream

Cream is the yellowish coloured fat from milk. The fat can be removed and made into different types of cream:

- single cream: this is white and thin, slightly thicker than milk and 20% fat. It does not thicken. It is used to add richness to some dishes, such as curries, and is also served with desserts
- whipping cream: this is off-white in colour, thicker than single cream and is 30% fat. It does thicken when whipped, and is used as a topping or for filling products, for example, choux buns and mousse
- double cream: this is 48% fat. It has a slightly thicker consistency than single cream but whips well to provide a very thick cream that can be used for piping on cakes and desserts. It is easy to over-whip double cream so it becomes too thick
- clotted cream: this is a thick, rich, yellowish cream which normally has a skin on it. The cream is made by heating milk until a thick layer of cream sits on top. This is then cooled and the cream removed. It is usually served with scones and jam
- crème fraiche: this is a mature, thick cream which has a slightly sharp but creamy flavour. It is available in different thicknesses. It is used as a topping for desserts or added to cooked sauces and soups.

Milk

Milk is a common and popular product around the world. It is available in many different forms:

- full-cream milk: this contains about 3.25% fat and has a creamy flavour
- semi-skimmed milk: some of the fat is removed from full-cream milk, to leave milk that is about 1.8% fat. It is white in colour and has a less creamy flavour than full-cream milk
- skimmed milk: most of the fat is removed to leave about 0.1% fat. Skimmed milk has a bland flavour and a watery, white colour
- Channel Island milk: this is a rich milk containing 5.5% fat, and has a very creamy flavour
- sterilised milk: this is heat-treated to make it last longer. The heating process alters the taste, smell and colour of the milk
- condensed milk: some of the water content is removed and replaced with sugar, which produces a very sweet, thick milk which is used in the confectionery industry
- powdered milk: this is milk which has been partly evaporated and then heated quickly to remove additional water. When required for use it needs to be rehydrated with water. The evaporation/heating process affects the colour and flavour
- soy milk: this is not made from an animal but is produced by soaking, crushing and cooking soy beans. Once filtered this is sold as soy milk. It looks like milk but has a very different flavour.

Yoghurt

Yoghurt (yogurt) is simply milk to which bacteria have been added. There are two main types of yoghurt:

- stirred yoghurt: the milk is fermented in large containers where it is stirred before being put into pots
- set yoghurt: the milk ferments in the pot.

There are many different varieties and flavours now available:

- bio-yoghurts: these are made with a special type of bacteria which have a good effect on the digestive system
- low-fat yoghurts: these are made with reduced-fat milk.

Fromage frais is often considered a yoghurt but is in fact made from fermented milk. Rennet and bacteria are added to milk which causes the milk to set. It is then stirred until a creamy consistency is achieved. Fromage frais can have fruits and flavours added to it, or can be natural. Natural fromage frais is used as an alternative to cream in some recipes.

For you to do

7 Visit the Cheese website and find out about other cheeses. In particular, find out about the following cheeses, making notes on the country of origin, the type of cheese, and giving a description of each:

a Adelost

b Bryndza

c Lebbene

d Caboc.

Your teacher may provide a small sample of different types of cheese for you to taste as well as giving an indication of the price.

Describe the appearance of each cheese, write down the price, and then rate the cheese for flavour. Give 5 marks if you like it a lot and only 1 mark if you do not like it. Which cheese do you prefer? Explain why.

Links to this site and other websites relating to Intermediate 2 Hospitality can be found at: www.leckieandleckie.co.uk by clicking on the Learning Lab button and navigating to the Intermediate 2 Hospitality Course Notes page.

Cereals

Some of the most popular cereals around the world are described below.

Barley

Barley grows in a range of different climates. It was one of the earliest cereals to be cultivated, and is available in many different forms:

- whole, pot or Scotch barley: the outer husk is removed before being soaked and then used in soups and stews
- pearl barley: the husk is removed and the grain is steamed, and processed. It is used to thicken soups and stews
- barley flour: this is ground and powdered pearl barley. It is used for thickening soups and stews as well as for some types of baking
- barley flakes: these are pressed and flattened barley grains. They are used to make milk puddings or as a topping for sweet and/or savoury foods.

Buckwheat

Although buckwheat is used as a cereal, it is actually the fruit of a plant related to the rhubarb family. The grain is triangular in shape and is popular in Russia (used to make porridge called kasha) and Japan (used to make a type of noodle called soba). Buckwheat grain is often roasted lightly to give a stronger flavour and colour. Buckwheat is available in many different forms, including buckwheat flour, which is added to traditional flours when baking to give a different flavour and texture to baked goods.

Corn

Corn is also known as sweetcorn and as maize. It can be used as a vegetable (in the form of sweetcorn), or the dried grains can be used to make cornflakes or popcorn. Corn is available in different forms:

- corn flour: a finely ground, white powder that is made from the corn kernels or nibs. This is used as a thickening agent in sauces and stews
- corn meal: a flour made from corn which can be added to soups, pancakes and muffins. It is also used to make polenta, a product used in Italian cookery.

Millet

'Millet' is the term used to describe the seeds of grasses that are found in Africa and Asia. Examples include common millet, sorghum, kaffir and bulrush millet. Millet has a delicate flavour and the grains tend to be pale yellow in colour. The grains need to be cracked before cooking so that they can absorb water. Millet grains can be used in the same way as rice. Millet is available as flour (used in baking and also in some types of pasta) and flakes (used for making porridge or added to muesli).

Oats

Oats are grown throughout the world. Once very popular in Scotland, wheat has replaced it as the most popular cereal. Oats can be found in many different forms:

- oatmeal: cut or ground oats, available in different grades. Traditionally used to make porridge it can also be used in bread making, baking (oatcakes) and as a thickening agent (stews)
- rolled oats or oat flakes: oat grains are treated with steam and flattened between rollers. This process produces quick-cooking oats that are used for porridge and for baked items (flapjacks)
- oat bran and oat germ: these are fine brown powders which are added to flour when baking bread, can be used to make a thin porridge, or can be sprinkled over savoury foods for flavour.

Quinoa

Quinoa is the very small, delicately flavoured golden seed of a small plant from South America. Quinoa is used in a similar way to rice and is very quick and easy to prepare. It is cooked in salted boiling water for 10–15 minutes before being drained and served along with stews and curries or used as an ingredient for stuffing items such as peppers.

Rice

Rice is one of the most important cereal products throughout the world. It is an aquatic plant grown in wet conditions in countries such as China and India. Rice comes in different forms:

- long grain: the grains are usually four times as long as they are wide, and the rice is traditionally used for savoury dishes
- medium grain: the grain is three times as long as it is wide, and the rice is used for both sweet and savoury dishes
- short grain: this is traditionally used for sweet dishes, such as rice pudding
- arborio rice: this is short grain rice that is used to make risotto.

There are different rice varieties, each with their own particular flavours and aromas, including white rice, brown rice and quick-cook rice. Also available are rice flakes (grains which have been processed into flakes, so they cook very quickly, and are used for milk puddings or as a thickening agent in soups), and ground rice (used in milk puddings or added to biscuit mixtures to provide a crisp texture).

Rye

Rye is a tough cereal that is grown in cold and harsh climates. The grain is hard and brown and has a slightly sour flavour. Rye comes in different forms:

- rye grains: often added to soups and stews
- rye flour: grains that have been ground, used to make rye bread or special rye biscuits.

Spelt

Spelt is a Middle-Eastern cereal that is similar to wheat. Spelt has a very nutty, wheaty flavour, and is used for making bread and pasta as well as cookies and crackers.

Wheat

Wheat has been grown for thousands of years and is one of the most common and popular cereals throughout the world. Wheat is most often turned into flour and used to make bread, cakes, pastries and biscuits as well as pasta. It is also available in other forms:

- wheat grains: these can be cooked and added to stews
- Bulgar wheat: the grains are part-cooked before being cracked, providing a light-textured grain that only needs to be rehydrated before being used. Sometimes used as an alternative to rice
- semolina: this is a yellow grain-type product made from hard wheat and is used to make milk puddings or to make pasta
- couscous: this is made from semolina grains which have been rolled, moistened and coated with wheat flour. Couscous is widely used in the Middle-East as an alternative to rice.

Wild rice

Wild rice is not actually rice; it is in fact the seed of an aquatic grass. It has a long, dark grain which is cooked in the same way as rice. Sometimes it added to rice mixtures that can be bought in supermarkets. It is much more expensive than normal rice and has a very distinctive, nutty flavour.

For you to do

8 Breakfast is an important part of the day. Visit the Eatwell website and answer the following questions.

   a Why is breakfast regarded as an important part of the diet?

   b Many teenagers miss breakfast because they say they do not have enough time. List three things a teenager could do to make sure that they do not miss out on breakfast.

Links to this website and other websites relating to Intermediate 2 Hospitality can be found at: www.leckieandleckie.co.uk by clicking on the Learning Lab button and navigating to the Intermediate 2 Hospitality Course Notes page.

LECKIE&LECKIE
Learning Lab

Peas, Beans and Pulses

There are many types of peas, beans and pulses used throughout the world. They are an important source of protein in diets which are low in animal food sources.

Aduki bean

Also called adzuki beans, these are small, red-brown beans, with a cream-coloured stripe. They are round in shape, and are slightly pointed at one end. They have a strong, nutty, sweet flavour. Aduki beans probably originate from China.

Black bean

Black beans are small balls (about the size of a pea) and are black in colour. They have cream-coloured flesh inside and a mild, sweet taste and a soft texture. The black bean originates in Central America and Mexico. Note: this is not the bean that is used to make black bean sauce common in Chinese cookery.

Black-eye bean

This is a kidney-shaped bean which has a creamy colour with a black spot. Black-eye beans have a distinctive savoury flavour with a dry, creamy texture. Originally native to Africa, they are widely grown in many Asian countries, and are used in many Indian curries.

Butter bean

Also known as the Lima bean, this is a large kidney-shaped bean. Butter beans have a buttery, floury texture and a subtle flavour that makes them useful for many dishes. The beans are generally cream or green in colour, although some varieties can be white, red, purple, brown or black.

Chickpea

The chickpea is also called chana or ceci bean. It is pale brown and is cooked whole. When cooked, it has a firm texture and adds colour and a nutty flavour to dishes.

Haricot bean

This is a small white bean, sometimes called the Navy bean. The haricot bean is used to make baked beans. It is a small, oval, creamy coloured bean, which if purchased dried, must be soaked and cooked before being used. Haricot beans have a coarse texture and delicate flavour.

Lentils

Belonging to the pulse family, lentils are the seeds of a plant. The seeds vary in size, shape and colour, so there are many different varieties. Lentils do not need to be soaked before cooking. They are a popular vegetarian food and are often served in winter soups and casseroles because they are very filling and are high in protein. Two common types of lentil are:

 green lentils: also called Puy lentils, these are small seeds with a meaty, peppery flavour. Green lentils are bigger than red lentils, and they hold their shape well during cooking

- red lentils: these are small orange-coloured seeds which have their outer skin removed and are then split in half. Red lentils have a delicate, nutty flavour and are often used to make soups and stews as well as spicy dhals (an Indian dish).

Mung bean

Whole mung beans are small, yellowish-green beans. They can also be bought as split beans. The whole beans are quite different from the split ones, and have a stronger flavour. In India, they are cooked with a variety of spices and other vegetables to make delicious dhals and curries.

Pinto bean

Pinto beans have a dark creamy colour with reddish brown specks of colour ('pinto' means 'painted' in Spanish). When cooked, the coloured specks disappear, and they become a pink colour.

Red kidney beans

As their name suggests, red kidney beans are shiny, fat, red, kidney-shaped beans which have a slightly meaty flavour. Kidney beans originate from Central and South America.

Soya bean

Soya beans originate from East Asia. For more than 5000 years they have been an important protein source for millions of people. Although soya beans are generally yellow, there are other varieties which are black, brown or green. Soya beans have a mild, nutty flavour.

Hints and tips

Hygiene and food safety tip

! Some beans can be very poisonous. Dried beans, particularly red kidney beans and soya beans, must be soaked for at least 8 hours and then cooked for a minimum of 10 minutes.

For you to do

9 Pulses are seeds such as beans and peas which are cooked and eaten. They contain lots of protein, so they are good for vegetarians who miss out on the protein provided by animal products. (Animal products are a common source of protein in the diet of non-vegetarians.)

Using the internet, find a recipe suitable for a vegetarian who does not eat meat, fish, eggs or cheese. The recipe should use chickpeas as the main ingredient.

Breads

There are many different types of bread from different parts of the world. This list describes only some of the breads found in different countries.

Bagel

The bagel is made of yeast and wheat flour, made into a dough which is then boiled in water and baked. These ring-shaped rolls have a dense, chewy texture. Bagels are usually served at breakfast. They are usually sliced open, toasted, and spread with cream cheese. Raisins, blueberries, onions, seeds or herbs can be added to the dough for extra flavour.

Bolillo

These are crusty Mexican sandwich rolls. A bolillo is a type of bread traditionally made in Mexico, El Salvador, Portugal and Brazil. In some parts of Mexico it is also known as 'Pan de Agua' (water bread). It is about 15cm long and is oval-shaped. It has a crunchy crust but is soft inside.

Breadsticks

Also known as grissini, breadsticks are long, thin sticks of crispy, dry bread. They were originally made in Turin and the surrounding area in Italy, and are thought to have been first created in the 14th century. Italians serve these crunchy breadsticks before meals as an appetiser. They can be plain or flavoured with, for example, sesame seeds, garlic, onion or herbs.

Brioche

A brioche is a very rich French bread, with a high egg and butter content, which give the bread a rich and tender texture. Brioche have a dark, golden, flaky crust, which is the result of an egg wash applied before and after the bread dough rises.

Ciabatta

Ciabatta is a rustic Italian bread with a heavy crust and a dense texture. It is a white bread made with wheat flour and yeast. The loaf is long, broad and flattish ('ciabatta' is the Italian word for 'slipper'). Ciabatta can be used for sandwiches. A toasted sandwich made from small loaves of ciabatta is known as a panino or panini.

Croissant

Croissants are French crescent-shaped rolls, made with puff pastry. They are very rich and tender. Croissant pastry can be flavoured with almond or chocolate before it is baked (if it has a chocolate filling it is called 'pain au chocolat'). Cooked croissants can be sliced and different sweet or savoury fillings added.

Crumpet

A crumpet is type of bread (or cake) made from flour and yeast. It is eaten mostly in the UK. In Scotland, the term is used for a large thin teacake, made from the same ingredients as a pancake. The crumpet is circular in shape, and has a distinctive flat top covered in small holes. It has a slightly spongy texture and a rather bland flavour.

Flat bread

There are many different varieties of flat bread throughout the world, including pitta (see below), chapattis, parathas, roti, tortilla and pancakes. They are especially common in India, the Middle and Far East and the Caribbean.

French bread

French bread is also known as a baguette, batarde or baton (the length of the bread determines its name). This is the traditional French bread that has a crunchy, dark brown crust and an open, chewy texture.

Kugelhopf

This German bread is a sweetened yeast bread with currants and almonds baked inside. It is usually shaped in a ring and served at breakfast.

Nan bread

Nan is a typical Indian bread made from white flour which is lightly leavened (raised). Nan is traditionally cooked in a Tandoor oven which gives the bread a light and slightly 'toasted' or charcoal flavour.

Pitta bread

Pitta is a flat bread from Greece and the Middle-East. It is the biggest selling ethnic bread in the UK. It is usually made from white flour but it can be made with wholemeal. Pitta bread is usually oval in shape and can form a pocket for fillings. Pitta bread is puffy and brown when newly cooked.

Pumpernickel bread

This Northern European bread is heavy and slightly sour. It is made with molasses (a form of sugar) and a blend of rye and wheat flours. It is often cut into thin slices and used for appetisers.

Rye bread

This is the favourite bread of North Europeans, who use it to make sandwiches. There are many different varieties of rye bread ranging from light tan to almost black. Pure rye bread contains only rye flour and no wheat flour. Rye and wheat flours are often used to produce a rye bread which has a lighter texture, colour and flavour than pure rye bread.

Wholemeal bread

A traditional UK bread, wholemeal bread uses most of the wheat grain during its manufacture. This gives the bread a dark colour and a nutty flavour.

For you to do

10 Complete the word search on different types of bread. Find these terms:

bagel	brioche	croissant
flour	French	grain
kugelhopf	loaf	Mexico
nan	oven	panini
rise	rye	yeast

L	A	O	F	B	A	J	K	U	G	E	L	X	O
C	T	O	E	A	U	C	Z	Q	R	G	U	T	C
H	E	G	W	G	X	Y	S	R	A	R	J	R	I
I	R	H	S	E	O	E	I	K	A	A	O	L	N
H	M	N	C	L	K	S	P	E	N	I	Z	V	F
O	C	M	T	O	E	T	A	A	S	N	K	W	R
I	T	M	N	I	I	L	Y	S	D	O	T	P	E
N	T	E	S	Q	U	R	A	S	D	M	C	V	N
I	X	X	N	A	M	N	B	P	E	E	R	I	C
N	V	I	E	W	T	T	K	G	T	C	O	Q	G
A	N	C	C	O	P	S	U	R	H	I	I	L	B
P	E	O	I	V	B	A	G	I	C	C	S	F	I
E	Y	R	Y	E	U	E	E	A	N	O	A	L	R
F	O	R	B	N	L	Y	L	N	E	S	N	O	E
D	J	S	U	E	R	T	H	C	R	P	T	G	S
U	B	N	A	N	R	L	O	A	F	A	A	T	M
G	I	Y	C	V	Z	K	P	M	T	B	R	D	E
X	N	I	N	A	P	O	F	L	O	U	R	N	S

CHAPTER 1
COOKERY SKILLS

1   Escoffier was born on 28 October 1846, and died 12 February 1935. He was born in a village called Villeneuve Loubet, near Nice. He began his training in his uncle's restaurant called *Le Restaurant Francais*, in Nice. In 1865 he moved to *Le Petit Moulin Rouge* in Paris. He wrote a number of important books including: *Le Traite sur L'art de Travailler les Fleurs en Cire* (1886); *Le Guide Culinaire* (1903); *Les Fleurs en Cire* (a new edition) (1910); *Le Carnet d'Epicure* (1911); *Le Livre des Menus* (1912); *Le Riz* (1927); *La Morue* (1929); *Ma Cuisine* (1934).

2   a   Use 12 level tablespoons or 4 heaped tablespoons.
    b   Use 8 level tablespoons.
    c   Use 1 teaspoon.
    d   Use 5 teaspoons or 1 tablespoon.
    e   Use $^1/_2$ a block of butter weighing 250g.
    f   Use 10 level tablespoons.
    g   Use $^1/_2$ teaspoon.

3   Equipment used in assembling the vegan spring roll: chopping board, small dish, finger or pastry brush, serving dish.

4   Put the vegetables in a large pan of boiling water. When the water comes back to the boil, then start timing the blanching. When time is up, drain and plunge the vegetables straight into iced water. When they are stone cold, drain and dry them on kitchen towel. Blanching times are: broccoli (cut into florets) – 2 minutes; parsnips (sliced) – 2 minutes; cabbage (sliced) – 1 minute.

5   a   Mango, pineapple juice, coconut milk, ice-cream.
    b   Mixing the frappé mix too much.
    c   The mixture will become thin, not the correct consistency.

6   a   Red onion.
    b   To keep the onion together, making it easier to dice.
    c   Sauces, chilli, marinara.

7   a   To loosen or lighten the mousse mixture prior to folding in the rest of the egg white.
    b   The mixture should be smooth and even coloured.

8   a   Prices range from £630 to £2200 (prices vary according to website referenced).
    b   Mincer and vegetable preparation attachments; bowl; beater; whisk; dough hook (features vary depending on the website used).
    c   Making bread and pizza dough; doner and meat mixes; cookie and biscuit dough; cake and sponge mix; batter; whipped cream; meringue; mayonnaise.

9   a   Beef.
    b   Red wine, vinegar, lemon juice, olive oil, pepper, salt, rosemary, garlic.
    c   Between 4 and 24 hours.

10 a   This list of soups is not exhaustive: split pea, red pepper, carrot, mushroom, fennel, pumpkin, leek, tomato, vegetable, chestnut.

b   Tomato purée – made of tomatoes that have been cooked briefly and strained, resulting in a thick liquid. Tomato paste – made of tomatoes that have been cooked for several hours, strained and reduced to a thick, rich concentrate. Tomato sauce – a thinner tomato purée, which may include other flavorings making it ready for use in other dishes and sauces.

11 a   This list is not exhaustive: cod, herring, salmon.
    b   This list is not exhaustive: carrots, apple, potatoes.

12 a   Mirepoix: to mix finely diced vegetables which, when fried in butter, are used as a base for brown sauces and stews.
    b   Concassé: to roughly chop.
    c   A la mode: beef pot roast, with fat, braised with vegetables and simmered in a sauce.
    d   Au jus: food served with its own juices or gravy.
    e   Entrée: this term can either mean the starter/appetiser or the main dish of a meal; normally with a sauce and garnish.
    f   Sabayon: a light creamy Italian custard.

13 a   To produce thin slices or shavings of vegetables such as carrots which can be used to create edible 'flowers'.
    b   To carve fruits and vegetables with different-sized 'chisel type' tools.
    c   To cut vegetables into different shapes, for example, turtle or butterfly.

15 Examples could include: breaded fish, scampi; cocktails, alcoholic drinks; pakora.

16 Chocolate leaves: brush a coating of melted chocolate on to the underside of a leaf, e.g. a rose leaf. Make sure the leaf is clean. The leaf should have strong defined veins that will show up better. Once the chocolate has cooled gently peel the leaf away, starting at the tip of the leaf.

Chocolate shells: these can be made from almost any shells. It is important to clean the shells thoroughly before use. You should also cover the shells with cling film before brushing on a thin covering of melted chocolate. Allow the chocolate to cool and then add a second thin layer. When the second layer has cooled the cling film can carefully be peeled off the chocolate, leaving the finished shell.

CHAPTER 2
FOOD PREPARATION FOR HEALTHY EATING

1 a Food such as bread, cereals, rice, pasta and potatoes.

  b Yes, these count as part of our required daily intake. If tinned, try to buy unsweetened varieties or those in natural fruit juice rather than in syrup.

  c Butter – food and drinks high in fat and/or sugar; eggs – meat, fish, eggs and beans; yoghurt – milk and dairy foods.

  d Foods such as beans, lentils and peas.

  e 4 portions – most women, most men and boys; 2 portions – girls/women who have not given birth or are pregnant/breastfeeding.

  f This is not an exhaustive list of examples: salmon, trout, mackerel, herring, sardines.

  g Fruit juice – 150ml; salad – 1 dessert bowl; grapes – handful.

  h Remove skin and any visible fat before cooking or before serving.

  i High sugar content can cause tooth decay; high sugar content means high in calories without providing nutritional benefits, and can contribute to individuals becoming overweight.

2 Suggestions could include: increase quantity of lasagne sheets slightly; increase amount of carrot, mushroom and celery slightly; use lean minced beef; omit bacon and add extra vegetables; don't use thickening agents (flour and butter) in stock; use poly-unsaturated fat instead of butter; use semi-skimmed or skimmed milk; use a smaller amount of mature cheddar cheese; use low-salt or salt alternative; omit oil used for browning mince.

3 a Milk is a good alternative to sugary fizzy drinks and semi-skimmed milk provides less fat than full-fat milk. The use of semi-skimmed milk is in line with existing recommendations, e.g. the Scottish Diet Action Plan.

  b Serving different types of fish provides variety in the menu. Oil-rich fish contain valuable, protective fatty acids that are deficient in the Scottish diet and their use should be encouraged. Many children are unfamiliar with these foods and should be encouraged to try them through the use of tasters.

  c Using these will help reduce fat intake, in line with the Scottish Diet Action Plan targets. As part of a healthy diet, it is also important to reduce the amount of saturated fats eaten, by replacing them with unsaturated fats with an emphasis on mono unsaturates. This is because saturated fats can contribute to heart disease. Saturated fats are found in many animal-based products such as meat, cheese and milk.

6 Organic products include: food; drink; clothing; cosmetics; health products; timber and wood products; compost; gardening supplies. Restaurants, bars, holiday accommodation, spas and shops can also carry an organic certification.

8

Cookery method	Fat content			Nutrient content	
	Increased	Maintained	Reduced	Maintained	Reduced
Stir-frying	Slightly			✔	
Steaming			Depending on the food	✔	
Braising				If served with cooking liquid	
Boiling		✔		If used for stock/gravy	Slightly
Stewing		✔		If served with cooking liquid	
Poaching		✔		✔	
Baking		✔		✔	
Roasting	Only if basted		✔	✔	
Grilling			✔	✔	

9

Times	Activities	Notes
1.00 – 1.05	Wash hands; collect ingredients.	
1.05 – 1.10	Prepare the chicken – wash, dab dry, cube.	
1.10 – 1.20	Prepare remaining ingredients for the dish: • green pepper – slice • red pepper – slice • carrots – batons • garlic – crushed • pineapple – drained.	
1.20 – 1.25	Clean work surface and wash dishes.	
1.25 – 1.30	Heat oil and brown chicken.	
1.30 – 1.35	Put water for rice on to boil. Add stir-fry ingredients and stir fry for 2 minutes.	See 1.10 – 1.20 above
1.35 – 1.45	Prepare the mixing sauce. Add rice to boiled water (1.40).	Rice ready at 1.55
1.45 – 1.50	Add the mixing sauce to the stir-fry and bring to boil.	
1.50 – 2.00	Clean table and wash and dry dishes. Drain rice at 1.55.	
2.00.	Serve Sweet and Sour Chicken with rice	

Note: time plans may vary slightly but there should be an appreciation of the importance of planning for cleaning work area and dishes, and for having the rice and stir-fry dish ready at the same time.

11 a, d   below 5°C

   b, c, f above 63°C

   e   above 82°C

12 Person drying hands on dish towel; person smoking in kitchen; person with dirty apron; cat eating food in kitchen; overfull rubbish bin; knocked over mug on work surface, with a spill dripping onto floor; cracked mixing bowl with mixture and a wooden spoon in it; uncovered cream cake with a fly sitting on it; fridge door left open; person has long hair which is not tied back.

CHAPTER 3
FOODS AND RECIPES FROM AROUND THE WORLD

1   The Lantern Festival or Yuanxiao Jie is a traditional Chinese festival, which is on the 15th of the first month of the Chinese New Year. The festival marks the end of the Chinese New Year celebrations. The traditional food is the glutinous rice ball called Yuanxiao or Tangyuan. This is a kind of sweet dumpling, made with sticky rice flour filled with sweet stuffing.

The Moon Festival is also known as the Mid-Autumn Festival and is one of the most important traditional events for the Chinese; it takes place on the 15th of the eighth lunar month. The Moon Festival celebrates the harvest, and is an occasion for family reunions. When the full moon rises, families get together to watch the full moon, eat traditional moon cakes, and sing moon poems.

2   New potatoes; green beans; lettuce; artichoke hearts; tomatoes; eggs; olives (black); tuna; balsamic vinegar; Dijon mustard; garlic; pepper; olive oil; basil; parsley; salt.

3   There are three well known methods of finding truffles. First is 'snuffling', where a pig sniffs about and reacts when it smells a truffle. Second, facing the bright sun, you can move the end of a stick over the ground, and if white flies fly straight up, you may find a truffle underneath the spot from which they took off. Finally, dogs can be trained to find truffles.

Making foie gras usually entails force-feeding geese or ducks. Starting several weeks prior to slaughter, a farmer inserts a tube down a bird's throat and then gorges the animal with corn gruel several times a day.

4   a   Vitamins.
    b   Snack
    c   A cactus that grows in the desert; it bears a red prickly pear fruit and the leaves can be cooked and eaten.
    d   The French opened French-style restaurants (serving French dishes, cheese, wine, liquors, and desserts), as well as pastry shops. The English introduced roast beef and tea. The Germans introduced coffee, tobasco (a hot spicy sauce) and different ways of using pork.

5   **Across:**
    3 Olive   6 Ramadan   8 Pomegranate
    10 Atlantic   11 Honey   12 Tagine   13 Shad
    Down:
    1 Ginger   2 Fez   4 Mint   5 Casablanca
    7 Couscous   9 Mechoui

6

K	M	A	R	J	O	R	A	M	C	G	W	Y	B	L
H	J	R	Y	O	Q	R	V	S	X	J	F	I	G	E
C	C	L	P	M	L	O	S	U	M	A	C	M	C	A
R	Q	O	W	T	U	C	T	M	A	H	L	A	B	B
K	J	T	E	O	E	K	S	A	L	L	C	S	N	C
Y	C	N	U	E	T	E	S	O	N	H	V	T	T	Q
N	N	G	P	H	C	T	H	Y	M	E	C	I	A	C
L	Z	N	K	J	I	O	J	R	G	C	P	C	R	I
N	U	T	M	E	G	R	C	D	I	L	L	K	R	N
H	Z	V	A	S	M	E	F	E	N	N	E	L	A	N
W	V	L	N	Z	H	G	W	N	M	R	Z	A	G	A
E	B	A	I	I	V	A	N	I	L	L	A	C	O	M
P	U	R	S	L	A	N	E	B	A	S	I	L	N	O
O	J	N	E	I	F	O	Z	W	W	C	O	D	V	N
C	Y	D	D	V	C	L	O	V	E	S	Y	K	T	O

CHAPTER 4
KEY INGREDIENTS

2 a Ginger: is an anti-oxidant; it relaxes blood vessels, stimulates blood flow, relieves pain, prevents nausea and sickness; may be useful in the prevention of heart disease, cancer, Alzheimer's disease and arthritis.

   b Turmeric: has anti-inflammatory properties, fighting inflammatory bowel disease, ulcerative colitis, rheumatoid arthritis, cystic fibrosis, cancer and Alzheimer's disease; may offer protection against heart and liver disease.

   c Cinnamon: has anti-clotting and anti-inflammatory properties and is an anti-oxidant; may help boost brain function; may have a role to play in regulating diabetes.

Note: these health benefits may not be fully researched and so should not be used as remedies for any of the diseases listed without first seeking medical advice.

3 a Durian: sometimes called the 'stinking fruit' because of the bad smell the fruit produces when it ripens. The durian tastes pleasant, however, like vanilla. Because of its unpleasant smell, it shouldn't be stored.

   b Xigua: a type of melon.

   c Ugli fruit: a citrus fruit which is a cross between a tangerine, a grapefruit and an orange. It is unattractive to look at, and sometimes has brown spots, but is easy to peel.

4 Peas, parsnips, potatoes, pak choi, parwal, palm hearts, peppers, pe tsai, pimento, pumpkin.

5 Other animals include: insects, cats (felines), dogs (canids), marsupials, reptiles, amphibians and primates.

6 a Finfish and shellfish.

   b One quarter.

   c Advantages include: provides a supply of fish that are naturally scarce in supply; farmed fish can be cheaper than seafish for the consumer to buy.

   d Disadvantages include: it is an inefficient method of producing fish; it can lead to pollution; it can lead to disease spreading from farmed fish to non-farmed fish; it can lead to cross-breeding between farmed and non-farmed fish; it can be uneconomic and wasteful as small fish are sometimes discarded.

7 a Adelost: is a creamy, semi-soft blue cheese from Sweden, made from cows milk. It has a drum shape with a pale cream, natural rind. It is lightly dusted with moulds and has evenly distributed streaks of blue-grey mould throughout. It has a sharp, salty tang, is 50% fat, and takes 2–3 months to ripen.

   b Bryndza: is a soft cheese made in Slovakia from ewes milk. It is cut into cubes and stored in brine, and takes about 4 weeks to mature. Fat content is around 45%.

   c Lebbene: is a soft cheese shaped into small balls made in Israel (and known elsewhere as Lebney in Syria, Labaneh in Jordan and Gibne in the Arabian Peninsula). It is made from sheep or goats milk, is eaten when very young (still almost liquid), and has a fat content of 45%.

   d Caboc: is a soft cheese made from cream-enriched cows milk in Scotland. It is shaped as a log and then rolled in toasted oatmeal, which gives it a nutty, yeasty flavour. It ripens in 5 days and has a fat content of 69%.

8 a When you wake up, your body has not had any food for several hours, so breakfast provides the energy you need in order keep going for the day ahead. Breakfast also provides essential vitamins and minerals.

   b Make a packed breakfast the night before and put it in the fridge for eating first thing in the morning; foods such as apples, pears, bananas, mini-bags of dried fruit and nuts and cartons of fruit juice are healthy and are ideal for eating on the go; if making a fruit salad for the evening meal, place any leftovers in a small plastic tub and eat this in the morning; breakfast and cereal bars can also be handy and quick to eat on the go, but these may be high in fat, salt and/or sugar.

9 There are many possible recipes available, but a suitable recipe would be potato and chickpea curry. This recipe can be found on the International Vegetarian Union website.

LECKIE&LECKIE
Learning Lab

10

L	A	O	F	B	A	J	K	U	G	E	L	X	O
C	T	O	E	A	U	C	Z	Q	R	G	U	T	C
H	E	G	W	G	X	Y	S	R	A	R	J	R	I
I	R	H	S	E	O	E	I	K	A	A	O	L	N
H	M	N	C	L	K	S	P	E	N	I	Z	V	F
O	C	M	T	O	E	T	A	A	S	N	K	W	R
I	T	M	N	I	I	L	Y	S	D	O	T	P	E
N	T	E	S	Q	U	R	A	S	D	M	C	V	N
I	X	X	N	A	M	N	B	P	E	E	R	I	C
N	V	I	E	W	T	T	K	G	T	C	O	Q	G
A	N	C	C	O	P	S	U	R	H	I	I	L	B
P	E	O	I	V	B	A	G	I	C	C	S	F	I
E	Y	R	Y	E	U	E	E	A	N	O	A	L	R
F	O	R	B	N	L	Y	L	N	E	S	N	O	E
D	J	S	U	E	R	T	H	C	R	P	T	G	S
U	B	N	A	N	R	L	O	A	F	A	A	T	M
G	I	Y	C	V	Z	K	P	M	T	B	R	D	E
X	N	I	N	A	P	O	F	L	O	U	R	N	S

Glossary

à la mode served with ice cream (p. 23)

anti-oxidant a substance which slows down the rate at which something decays because of a reaction with oxygen (p. 30)

appetiser a small amount of food eaten before a meal (p. 90)

aquatic living or growing in water (p. 115)

artificial sweetener a man-made substance which has a similar taste to sugar (p. 33)

assemble to bring together; the last stage in food preparation (excepting garnishing and decoration) (p. 14)

au jus a sauce (p. 23)

avocado a tropical fruit with thick green or purple skin and oily, green, edible flesh which has a large seed at the centre (p. 75)

baguette a long, thin, white loaf of bread; French in origin (p. 120)

bake dry method of cooking in which prepared food is cooked in a pre-heated oven (p. 41)

baste to spoon cooking juice over meat as it cooks, adding flavour and retaining moisture (p. 42)

Béchamel a white sauce (p. 9)

blanch dip food into boiling water for a short time before cooling quickly (p. 15)

blend combine two or more ingredients together to form a smooth paste (p. 16)

blitz to make into small pieces (p. 20)

boil wet method of cooking in which prepared food is cooked in boiling liquid (p. 43)

bouillabaisse fish stock (p. 68)

bouquet garni French term for a bundle of herbs tied together and used to flavour foods cooking in a liquid. (p. 35)

braise wet method of cooking food slowly in a covered dish in a little fat and liquid (p. 43)

brigade (system) people who work together in the preparation and cooking of food, with specific roles (pp. 6–7)

broth a thin soup often with vegetables and rice in it (pp. 59, 60)

brown the process of making food brown by cooking it (p. 48)

brunoise term for production of small, diced food items; French in origin (p. 23)

calorie a unit of energy, used to measure the amount of energy found in food (p. 30)

campaign organise a series of activities to get something done (p. 28)

canapé a small, thin biscuit or piece of bread which has a savoury food on top (p. 10)

canteen a place in a factory, office or school where food and meals are sold, often at a lower than usual price (p. 39)

caterer person who provides and sometimes serves food (p. 28)

cereal a type of grass which produces grains or seeds that are used as a food source (p. 29)

Chef de partie chef in charge of a section of work in a kitchen (p. 8)

chinois a strainer (p. 22)

chop cut into pieces (p. 17)

churn to mix or stir milk or cream until it becomes butter (p. 110)

citrus fruit the fruit of citrus trees with bitter peel and acidic, juicy flesh, e.g. oranges, lemons, limes (p. 101)

Commis chef assistant cook to the Chef de partie (p. 8)

components ingredients in a recipe (p. 46)

concassé cookery term meaning to roughly chop (p. 23)

confectionery small pieces of sweet food made from sugar or chocolate (p. 33)

congee a type of rice porridge that is eaten in many Asian countries (p. 60)

conical cone-shaped (p. 22)

contaminant a substance that spoils the purity of something or makes it poisonous (p. 48)

continental breakfast a simple meal consisting of fruit juice, coffee and bread with butter and jam (p. 67)

contingency something that might happen in the future, usually causing problems or making further changes necessary (p. 46)

croûton a small square piece of bread that is fried or toasted and which is added to soup or salad just before serving (p. 35)

cure to preserve using salt or smoke (p. 105)

dash a small amount (p. 13)

debris broken or torn pieces of something larger (p. 22)

decorate add something to sweet food to make it more attractive (pp. 14, 24)

deputise stand in for someone who is generally regarded as being the more senior (p. 10)

dhal a thick spicy stew typical of Indian and Pakistani cookery, made from pulses, e.g. lentils (p. 100)

dice cut food into small squares (p. 18)

dot place small bits of something such as fat over the surface of food (p. 13)

dough a stiff mixture of flour, liquid and other ingredients that can be worked with the hands (p. 19)

drizzle pour liquid slowly over something, especially in a thin line or small drops (p. 87)

dry method (of cooking) cooking that does not require a liquid (p. 41)

dust cover something with a fine powder (p. 13)

Eatwell plate a visual guide to understanding healthy eating, produced by the Food Standards Agency (p. 29)

eggplant an oval purple vegetable which is white inside and which is usually eaten cooked; also known as an aubergine. (pp. 61, 89, 103)

entrée starter or appetiser; in some countries it is the main dish of a meal (p. 23)

ethics a set of beliefs which guide behaviour (p. 67)

evaporated (milk) milk that has been thickened or dried by removing some or all of the water (p. 112)

farinaceous made from, rich in or consisting of flour or starch (p. 10)

fast eat no food (p. 80)

fertiliser a natural or chemical substance which is spread on the land or given to plants to make them grow well (p. 39)

fibre a type of material in fruit, vegetables and cereals that adds bulk to the diet and helps digestion (p. 30)

filo pastry very thinly rolled, almost transparent pastry (pp. 89, 92)

foie gras a popular French delicacy made from duck or goose liver (p. 67)

fold gently mix ingredients together with a metal spoon to prevent air loss (p. 18)

fromage frais a type of soft, pale cheese which is low in fat, and to which flavours are often added (p. 33)

game wild animals and birds that are hunted for food (p. 9)

garnish decorate a savoury dish (pp. 14, 24)

gram metric unit of measurement, used to measure mass; equal to 0.001 kilograms (p. 11)

grill dry method of cooking food under direct heat (p. 41)

guidelines information which advises people on how something should be done. (p. 28)

haute cuisine cooking of a high standard, typically French cooking (p. 66)

Head chef chef in charge of a kitchen (p. 7)

hold to keep a food item at a particular temperature or in a particular state, e.g. frozen (p. 37)

hors d'oeuvre small savoury dish eaten at the start of a meal (p. 10)

immerse the process of placing an item completely under the surface of a liquid (p. 24)

infestation state of being overrun by pests, e.g. insects, rodents, birds (p. 55)

insecticide a chemical substance made and used for killing insects, especially those which eat plants (p. 39)

jardinière food preparation process that produces thin strips of vegetables, like batons (p. 23)

julienne food preparation process that produces very thin strips of vegetables, like matchsticks (p. 23)

kilogram metric unit of measurement, used to measure mass; equal to 1000 grams (p. 11)

kitchen hygiene hygiene relating to the kitchen environment, i.e. where food is prepared and/or cooked (pp. 54–55)

knead process of handling a dough when making bread or pastry (p. 19)

knobbly having lumps on the surface (p. 103)

leach the process of substances such as minerals moving from a food item into a liquid, e.g. stock (p. 37)

lean lacking in fat (p. 32)

litchi fruit with a rough brown shell and sweet white flesh; also known as lychee (p. 61)

litre metric unit of measurement, used to measure volume; equal to 1000 millilitres (p. 11)

longan a subtropical fruit very similar to litchi (p. 61)

lotus paste crushed seeds of the lotus plant used in Asian cookery (p. 60)

macedoine (French) cooking term for diced mixed vegetables (p. 23)

marinade a mixture of oil, wine and herbs added to food before cooking in order to add flavour, colour and/or to soften texture (p. 19)

marinate to flavour food by covering with herbs, spices, oils or other highly flavoured ingredients and liquids (p. 19)

membrane thin layer of material surrounding or protecting a delicate object, e.g. an orange segment (p. 21)

microwave a short electromagnetic wave used for cooking food (p. 42)

millilitre metric unit of measurement, used to measure volume; equal to 0.001 litres (p. 11)

mirepoix (French) term for mixture of onions, carrots and celery (p. 23)

mise en place advanced food preparation (p. 8)

mollusc any animal which has a soft body and no spine, e.g. oyster (p. 109)

mono-unsaturated acid a type of fatty acid, generally regarded to be less of a health risk than other fatty acids (p. 33)

muslin finely woven cotton fabric (p. 22)

mycoprotein product often used by vegetarians as an alternative to meat (p. 32)

nouvelle cuisine French cookery which uses a lighter approach to food cooking and presentation than traditional haute cuisine (p. 66)

nutrient a chemical substance which plants and animals need in order to live and grow (p. 37)

obesity a condition of being extremely fat (p. 33)

olive oil a yellow or green oil obtained by pressing ripe olives (p. 88)

organic not using artificial chemicals in the growing of plants and animals for food and other products (p. 39)

ounce imperial unit of measurement, used to measure mass; equivalent to approximately 25 grams (p. 11)

palette knife blunt knife used for shaping or turning foods (p. 14)

parsley en branche (French) term for a large sprig of parsley (p. 27)

partie system system for organising an industrial kitchen (pp. 6–7)

pass change from one state to another, e.g. from a solid to a liquid (p. 20)

pâté a thick or smooth soft savoury mixture made from meat, fish or vegetables (p. 39)

paysanne (French) term for the preparation of vegetables normally into thin slices, cubes or triangles (p. 23)

personal hygiene hygiene relating to the chef or cook (pp. 53–54)

petit four a small cake or biscuit, usually served at the end of a meal with coffee (p. 10)

pilaf (pilaff) a Middle Eastern or Asian dish made from a grain such as rice usually with a broth and a variety of meat or vegetables (p. 89)

pinch a small amount of an ingredient, e.g. powder, usually the amount a person can hold between their first finger and thumb (p. 13)

pith the white substance found between the skin and the flesh of citrus fruits such as oranges (p. 21)

planetary mixer industrial food mixer (p. 19)

poach wet cooking method in which food is gently cooked in liquid (p. 44)

polenta dish made from boiled cornmeal (p. 114)

poly-unsaturated acid a type of fatty acid, generally regarded to be less of a health risk than other fatty acids (p. 33)

portion the amount of a particular food that is served to one person (p. 25)

pot roast dry cooking method in which food is cooked slowly in a covered dish with a small amount of liquid and sometimes vegetables (p. 42)

potwash term for a kitchen assistant (p. 9)

pound imperial unit of measurement, used to measure mass; equal to approximately 454 grams (p. 11)

process step that has to be undertaken to complete a task (p. 46)

promote encourage something to happen (p. 28)

pulses seeds such as beans or peas which are cooked and eaten (p. 31)

purée make a smooth thick paste (p. 20)

Ramadan a holy month in the Muslim year during which Muslims fast (have no food or drink) during the day (p. 80)

ramekin a small dish in which food for one person is baked and served (p. 68)

ratatouille a savoury dish made by cooking vegetables in a liquid over a slow heat (p. 68)

refresh to help bring back to a previous healthy state (p. 15)

rehydrate to add water to a dried product to return it to nearly its original state (p. 112)

reputation the opinion that people in general have about someone or something (p. 10)

resinous having a thick and sticky texture (p. 102)

responsibility control or authority one person has over someone or something (p. 10)

roast dry cooking method in which food is cooked in an oven or over a fire (p. 42)

rub in mix fat and flour together using the fingertips to obtain a breadcrumb-like mixture (p. 20)

rustic simple and rough in appearance (p. 119)

sabayon a sweet or savoury sauce made by beating egg yolks over a simmering water (p. 23)

saturated a type of fatty acid, generally regarded to be more of a health risk than other fatty acids (p. 35)

sauerkraut cabbage which has been cut into small pieces and preserved in vinegar (p. 69)

sauté cook food in oil and fat over heat, usually until it is brown (p. 71)

scant very little and not enough (p. 13)

scullery a place next to a kitchen where pans are washed and vegetables are prepared for cooking (p. 9)

seafood edible animals from the sea (p. 67)

sediment a soft substance that is like a wet powder, consisting of very small pieces of solid material which have fallen to the bottom of a liquid (p. 22)

segment divide something into different parts (pp. 21, 26)

simmer cook something in liquid at a temperature slightly below boiling (p. 43)

skin outer protective layer; to remove the skin of something (p. 21)

smoothie a thick cold drink made mainly from fruit, sometimes with milk, cream or yoghurt (p. 16)

sorghum a type of grain grown in hot countries (p. 61)

Sous chef assistant to the head chef (p. 7)

soya a small edible bean which is grown for use as a food for people and animals. Soya is often used as an alternative to meat (p. 32)

spatula a tool with a flat blade used in cooking for mixing, spreading or lifting food (p. 18)

squash a type of large vegetable with a hard skin and a lot of seeds at its centre (p. 75)

staple basic or main food or ingredient of a country (p. 81)

steam wet method of cooking where prepared food is cooked in steam (p. 44)

stew wet method of cooking where prepared food is cooked and served in a small amount of cooking liquid (p. 44)

stir-fry dry method of cooking where prepared food is cooked quickly in a small amount of oil (pp. 43, 59)

stock a liquid used to add flavour to food and which is made by boiling meat or fish bones or vegetables in water or other liquid (p. 43)

strain separate liquid food from solid food (p. 22)

subtropical belonging to parts of the world that have very hot weather (p. 102)

supreme remove the skin and membranes from a product, e.g. orange, chicken fillet (p. 21)

taco a hard, folded, thin flat bread usually filled with meat, cheese and hot spicy sauce; Mexican (p. 74)

tagine a Moroccan earthen cooking dish; the food prepared in a tagine (p. 81)

tamari a type of soy sauce produced in Japan (pp. 63–64)

taro root a type of root vegetable similar to a potato; used in Asian cuisine (p. 61)

task a piece of work to be undertaken or completed (p. 46)

taverna a Greek restaurant or eating place traditionally found by the sea (p. 88)

tofu a soft pale food which has very little flavour but is high in protein and is made from soya (pp. 32, 38)

tortilla a type of thin, round bread made from maize and eggs; Mexican (p. 74)

tropical belonging to parts of the world between the two tropics (p. 102)

truffle a type of edible fungus which is grown underground; it is very rare and expensive, and is considered a French delicacy (p. 69)

unsaturated a type of fatty acid, generally regarded to be less of a health risk than other fatty acids (p. 33)

vapour gas or extremely small drops of liquid which result from the heating of a liquid or solid (p. 44)

vegetarian a person who does not eat meat for health, religious, economic or moral reasons (p. 32)

vending machine machine that serves food or drink on payment of money (p. 39)

vol au vent a small, light, cup-shaped pastry case with a savoury sauce filling (p. 10)

wet method (of cooking) cooking that requires a liquid (p. 41)

wilt to become weak and lose structure/become very soft (p. 104)

wok Chinese pan used for frying food quickly (p. 59)

work plan (time plan) a schedule of timed activities to help the organisation of food production and cookery (p. 47)